Basic skills in geography

geography

Book 2

David Rose

OXFORD UNIVERSITY PRESS 1988

For the teacher

- *Basic Skills in Geography* deals with key geographical concepts by emphasizing skills.
- The course stresses an individualized, activities-based approach by highlighting graphic work.
- The scheme incorporates a diagnostic element.
- Book 2 teaches children about the structure of the world's environment and highlights its physical geography.

Using the book

The books in the scheme are divided into a number of units. A series of **key words** are highlighted in each unit, guiding the pupils through its content. These can be reinforced by the teacher in follow-up activities. **Exercises** are graded within each unit, to allow all pupils a degree of success, while extending the abilities of the more able. This allows a **diagnostic** element to be incorporated into the scheme, allowing specific weaknesses to show up more clearly.

Book 2 is divided into ten main units. Each unit deals with a key geographical concept or a particular skill, and develops it sequentially over a series of well-structured stages. It incorporates some of the skills highlighted in Book 1. These skills are reinforced, and developed to a higher level than was possible, or desirable, in the first book. In Book 2, all the skills are developed within the context of a theme based on general world geography. In addition, five new skills are introduced. These new skills incorporate concepts which are more appropriate to older pupils.

Four essential criteria govern the overall content in Book 2. Firstly, there is an emphasis on physical geography. Secondly, there is a strong element of place location. Thirdly, wherever possible, attempts have been made to relate the world geography theme to the experiences of the pupils. Finally Book 2 allows those skills introduced in Book 1 to be practised and reinforced in a different context.

For Andrew, Stuart and Laura

© Oxford University Press, Walton Street, Oxford OX2 6DP

Oxford New York Toronto
Delhi Bombay Calcutta Madras Karachi
Petaling Jaya Singapore Hong Kong Tokyo
Nairobi Dar es Salaam Cape Town
Melbourne Auckland
and associated companies in
Berlin Ibadan

Oxford is a trade mark of Oxford University Press

ISBN 0 19 833383 8

Typeset by Oxprint Ltd, Oxford
Printed in Hong Kong

Contents

How to do the work

This section shows you how to answer the questions in this book.

First look at these photographs:

Photograph 1
The countryside on Dartmoor, in Britain

Photograph 2
The countryside on St. Lucia in the West Indies

There are five main types of questions in this book. They are:

Type 1: True or false

If you think a sentence is correct, write *True*.
If you do not think it is correct, write *False*.

This type of exercise is shown by this sign **T/F**

T/F **Exercise A**

Look at Photograph 1. Write *True* or *False* for the sentences below. Do not copy the sentences.
Answer like this:

   1. True

1. Photograph 1 shows part of Dartmoor, in Britain.
2. There is a church in the photograph.
3. There is a lake in the photograph.
4. There is a big city in the photograph.
5. There is a forest in the photograph.

Type 2: Make your choice

In this type of question, you have to choose the correct answer. Only one of the answers is correct. You must copy the sentence so that it is correct.

These exercises are shown by the sign **CH**

Type 3: Matching

In this type of exercise you have to put together two parts of a sentence. You are given a list of beginnings. There is also a list of sentence endings. You must put the beginnings and the sentence endings together, to make full sentences.

These exercises are shown by the sign **M**

Sometimes you only have to match letters and words.

Type 4: Fill in the gaps

In this type of exercise you have to copy the sentences and put in the missing words, so it all makes sense.

These exercises are shown by the sign **FG**

Sometimes you are given the missing words.

Type 5: Finish the sentence

In this type of question you have to finish the sentence on your own.

These exercises are shown by the sign **FS**

There are other types of exercises. Some have no sign.

If they have the sign **T** see your teacher first.

CH **Exercise B**

Look at Photograph 2. Copy and complete the sentences below. Answer like this:

1. The photograph shows a part of St. Lucia in the West Indies.

1. The photograph shows a part of St. Lucia in the (West / South / North) Indies.
2. The West Indies looks a very (hot / cold / cool) place.
3. There are (two / no / one) cities in the photograph.
4. There are many (roads / trees / houses) in the photograph.

M **Exercise C**

Match the words below with their sentence endings. Answer like this:

1. Physical geography is about the shape of the land.

Vegetation / Climate / Physical / Continents

1. _____ geography is about the shape of the land.
2. _____ are very large areas of land.
3. _____ is the plant life of a place.
4. _____ is the average weather of a place.

FG **Exercise D**

Copy and complete the sentences using words from the list below:

The two photographs show two very different _____. Photograph 2 shows part of St. Lucia which has a _____, sunny climate. Photograph 1 shows part of Dartmoor in Britain, where not even the _____ is always hot.

summer / countries / hot

FS **Exercise E**

Copy and complete these sentences:

1. Dartmoor is a beautiful _____.
2. The vegetation in St. Lucia is _____.
3. The climates of Britain and the West Indies are _____.

Exercise F

1. Write a sentence about Photograph 1.
2. Write a sentence about Photograph 2.

Maps 1

Key words

direction   countries
compass

You will often need to use maps to tell the direction of places.
Direction on maps is shown by a compass.

This diagram names the points of a compass:

Imagine John is in the centre of the compass and he wants to move **towards** the north-east. He will walk in a line towards Beverley like this:

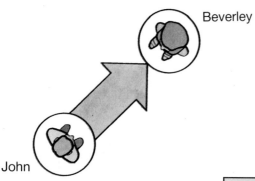

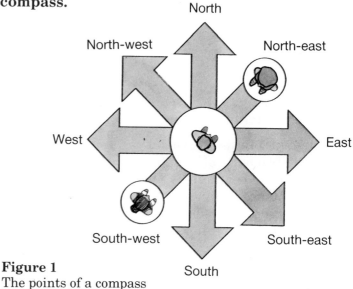

Figure 1
The points of a compass

Imagine John wants Julie to come to him. She will come **from** the south-west.

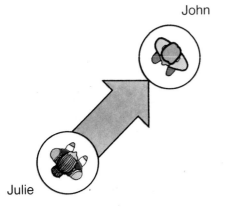

This wind has come from the west:

FG **Exercise A**

Copy the drawings and complete the sentences.

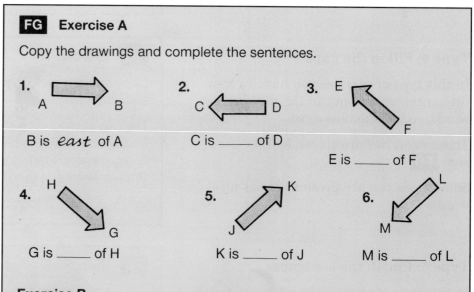

1. A ⟶ B

B is *east* of A

2. C ⟵ D

C is _____ of D

3. E ⬉ F

E is _____ of F

4. H ⬊ G

G is _____ of H

5. J ⬈ K

K is _____ of J

6. L ⬋ M

M is _____ of L

Exercise B

These drawings show where the wind is coming from.
Copy the drawings and name the direction the wind is coming from.
Like this:

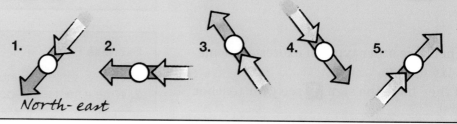

1. North-east
2.
3.
4.
5.

This map shows the countries of
Western Europe.

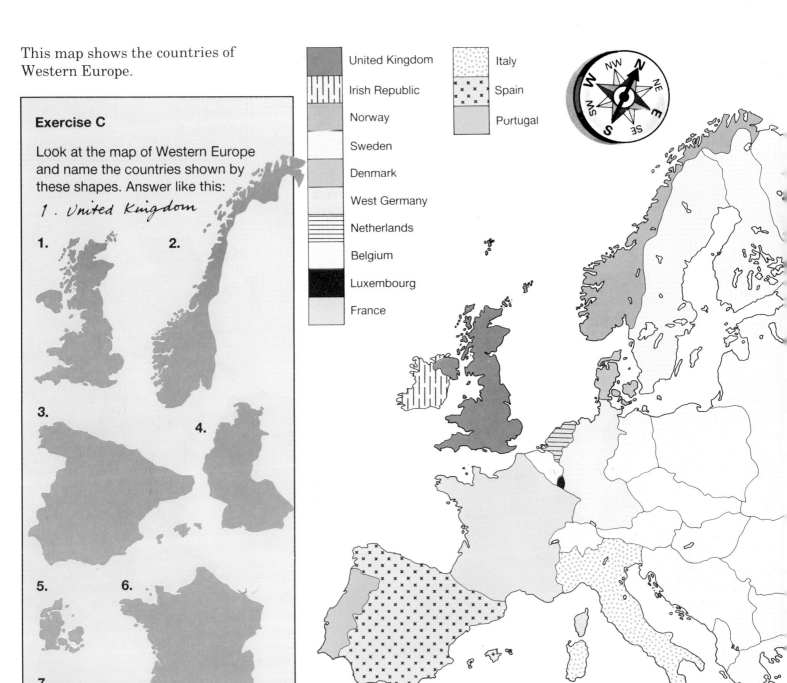

Exercise C

Look at the map of Western Europe
and name the countries shown by
these shapes. Answer like this:

1. United Kingdom

1.
2.
3.
4.
5.
6.
7.

United Kingdom
Irish Republic
Norway
Sweden
Denmark
West Germany
Netherlands
Belgium
Luxembourg
France

Italy
Spain
Portugal

Figure 2 Map of Western Europe

T/F Exercise D

Look at the map and write True or False.
Answer like this: *1. True*

1. Portugal is west of Spain.
2. Belgium is north-east of France.
3. Italy is south-east of Switzerland.
4. France is east of West Germany.
5. Spain is south-west of France.
6. The British Isles are west of Denmark.

Exercise E

1. Draw a map of your own, showing the shapes of
   six imaginary countries.
2. Colour each shape.
3. Give each shape a name.

Exercise F

Write six sentences, like those in Exercise D, to show
the directions between the countries you have drawn.

Maps 2

Maps are useful for showing temperatures. This section uses maps to look at the weather in Western Europe.

Figure 1
The British Isles

Figure 2
The British Isles showing summer temperatures

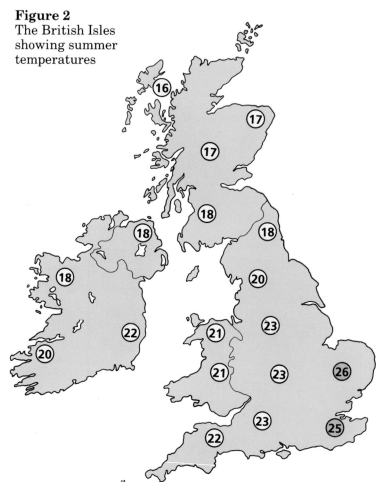

FG **Exercise A**

Look at the map of the British Isles in summer. Answer the questions below. Like this:

1. The temperature in South-west England is 22°C.

2. The temperature in South-east England is _____ °C.
3. The temperature in North-west Scotland is _____ °C.
4. The temperature in North-east Scotland is _____ °C.
5. The temperature in Central Wales is _____ °C.
6. The temperature in Northern Ireland is _____ °C.

CH **Exercise B**

Copy and complete these sentences:

1. The temperatures in the north of Scotland are (higher/lower) than in the south of England.
2. The temperatures in South-west England are (higher/lower) than in South-east England.
3. In summer, the warmest places are in the (south/north).

Exercise C

Look at Figure 1. Write five sentences about the directions of the countries. Like this:

1. Scotland is north of England.

The weather may change from day to day, but the pattern of weather may not change very much. The pattern of weather of a place is called its climate.

The summer temperatures in the British Isles are not usually very hot, and not nearly as hot as those in Southern Europe. The winter temperatures in the British Isles are not nearly as cold as those in Northern Europe or in Russia, Canada, or Northern China.

The temperatures throughout the British Isles are usually moderate. **The British Isles has a temperate climate**.

Most of Western Europe has a temperate climate too. Look at this map showing summer temperatures in Western Europe.

Figure 3 Western Europe showing summer temperatures

FG Exercise D

Look at the map of Western Europe. Write down the temperatures in these places. Answer like this:

1. England = 19°C, 20°C.

1. England	= _____	°C.
2. Portugal	= _____	°C.
3. Spain	= _____	°C.
4. Italy	= _____	°C.
5. Norway	= _____	°C.
6. Belgium	= _____	°C.
7. Denmark	= _____	°C.
8. Scotland	= _____	°C.
9. West Germany	= _____	°C.
10. France	= _____	°C.

Exercise E

1. Name the three hottest countries on the map of Western Europe.
2. Name the three coldest countries on the map of Western Europe.

Exercise F

Look at the map of Europe. Write five sentences about the weather in Europe in the summer.

T Exercise G

Look for photographs which show temperature or weather in different parts of Europe. If you can, find photographs in magazines, cut them out, stick them in your book and describe what each photograph shows.

Maps 3

Key words

mountains
rivers
oceans
continents

Maps can also show the positions of seas and oceans, rivers, lakes and mountains. These make up the physical geography of an area.

Look at this map showing the most important mountains, rivers and seas in Europe.

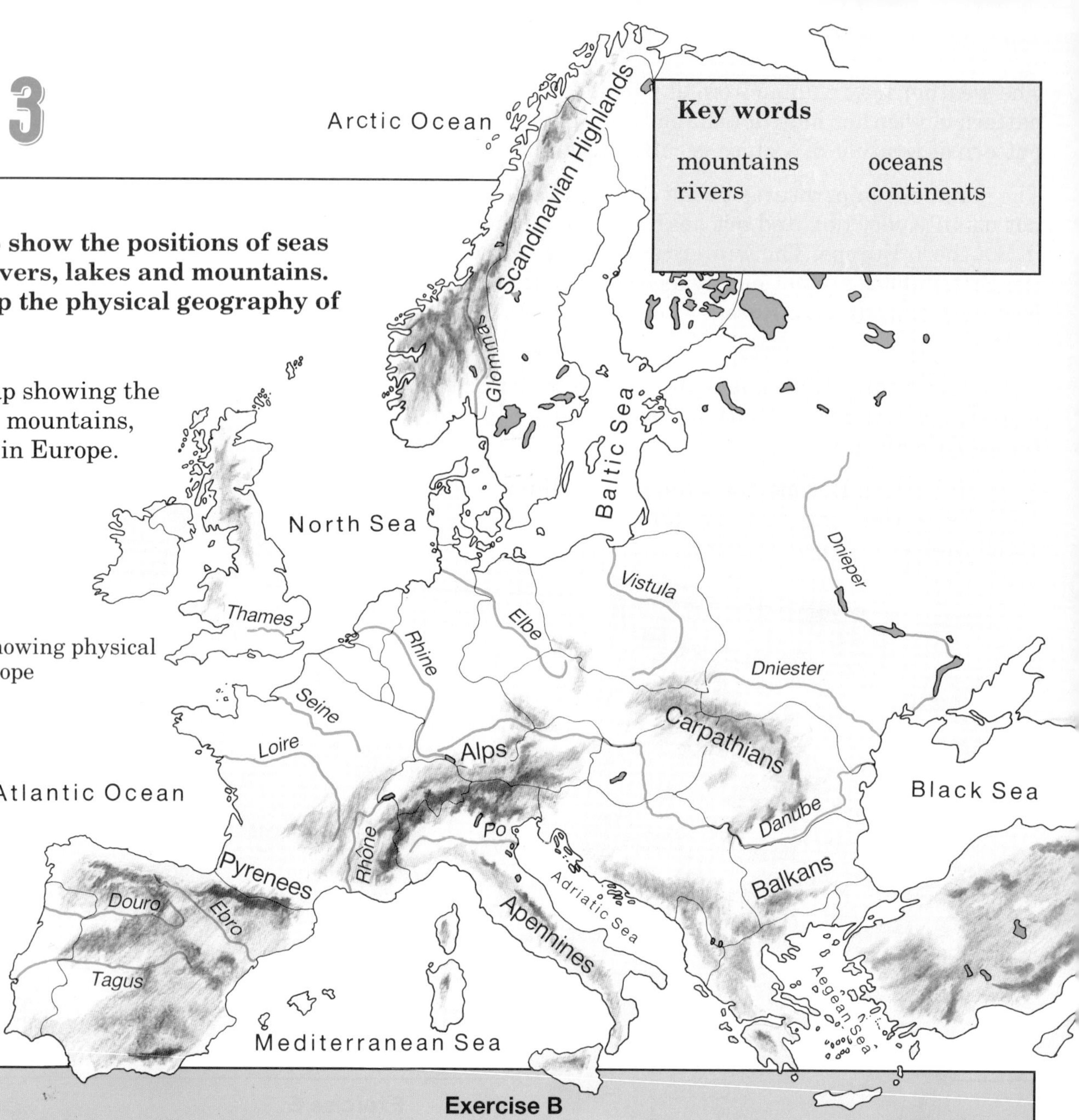

Figure 1 Map showing physical geography of Europe

Exercise A

1. Name the ocean to the west of Europe.
2. Name the sea to the south of Europe.
3. Name the ocean north of Europe.
4. Name a sea in the eastern part of Europe.

Exercise B

1. Name a river in West Germany.
2. Name a river in France.
3. Name a river in Italy.
4. Name a river in Portugal.

Exercise C

Name the mountains between Spain and France.

Exercise D

Choose any three mountain areas shown on the map, and for each one write a sentence to explain where it is in Europe.

Exercise E

Look at this chart for Italy.

	Italy
Mountains	*Apennines*
River	*Po*
Sea	*Mediterranean*

Choose a country on the map, and do a chart for the country you have chosen.

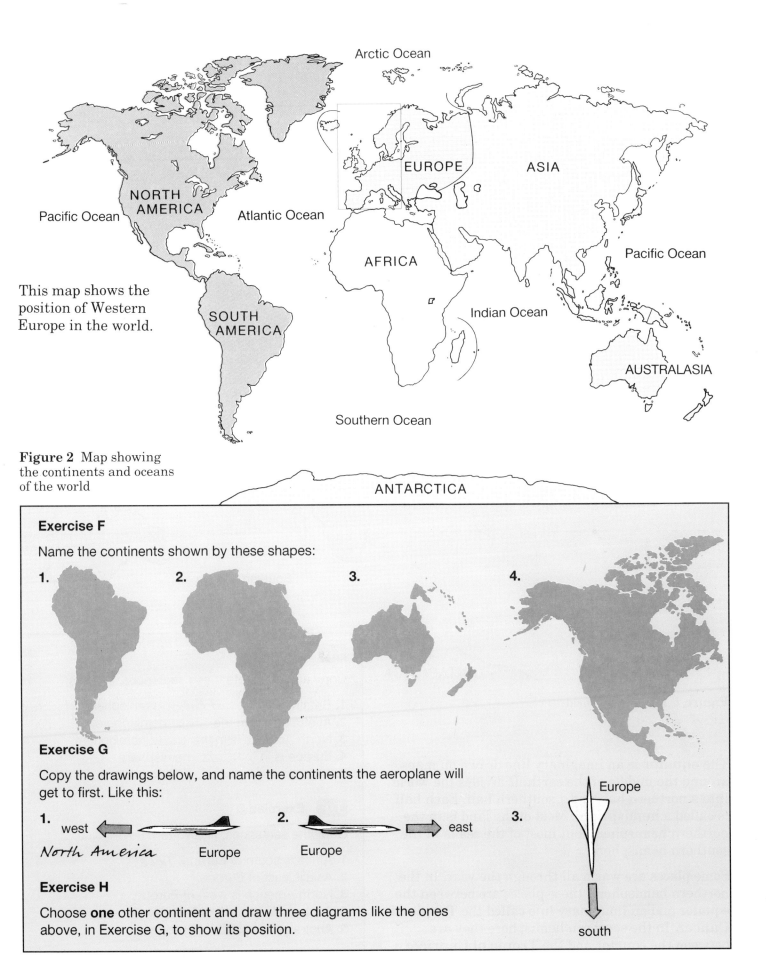

This map shows the position of Western Europe in the world.

Figure 2 Map showing the continents and oceans of the world

Exercise F

Name the continents shown by these shapes:

1.
2.
3.
4.

Exercise G

Copy the drawings below, and name the continents the aeroplane will get to first. Like this:

1. west ← [aeroplane] Europe
   North America

2. Europe [aeroplane] → east

3. Europe [aeroplane] ↓ south

Exercise H

Choose **one** other continent and draw three diagrams like the ones above, in Exercise G, to show its position.

Maps 4

Maps can contain a lot of information about temperature. So maps can show the coldest and hottest parts of the world, and the temperate parts of the world.

Map makers draw imaginary lines to divide up different parts of the world. Look at the lines drawn on this map that were not shown on the map on the page before.

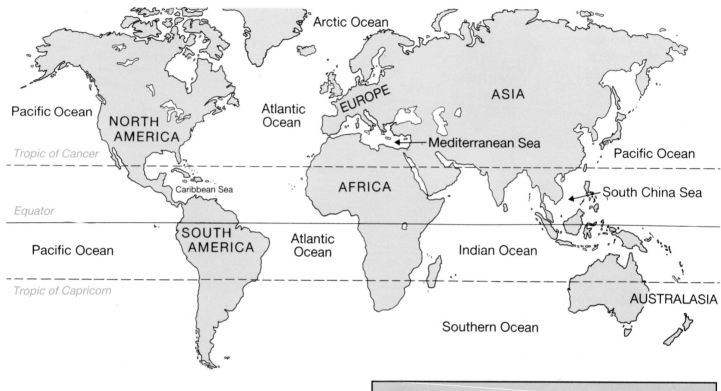

Figure 1 Map of the world

The **equator** is an imaginary line drawn on maps around the middle of the earth. It divides the world into a northern half and a southern half. Each half is called a **hemisphere**. Most of the land is in the northern hemisphere, but most of the sea is in the southern hemisphere.

Some places are warm all through the year. In the northern hemisphere, these places are between the equator and an imaginary line called the **Tropic of Cancer**. In the southern hemisphere they are between the equator and the **Tropic of Capricorn**.

FG   Exercise A

Copy and complete these sentences, like this:

1. Britain is in the *northern* hemisphere.
2. Australasia is in the _____ hemisphere.
3. North America is in the _____ hemisphere.
4. Europe is in the _____ hemisphere.
5. Antarctica is in the _____ hemisphere.

T/F   Exercise B

Copy the sentences, and write True or False.

1. Africa is south of Europe. *True*
2. Asia is east of Europe.
3. North America is west of Europe.
4. Australasia is north of Europe.
5. Australasia is south of Europe.

Look at this map of the world's different climates. The lines on the map make it look like a tidy jig-saw. In the real world, the change from one climate to another may happen gradually over hundreds of miles.

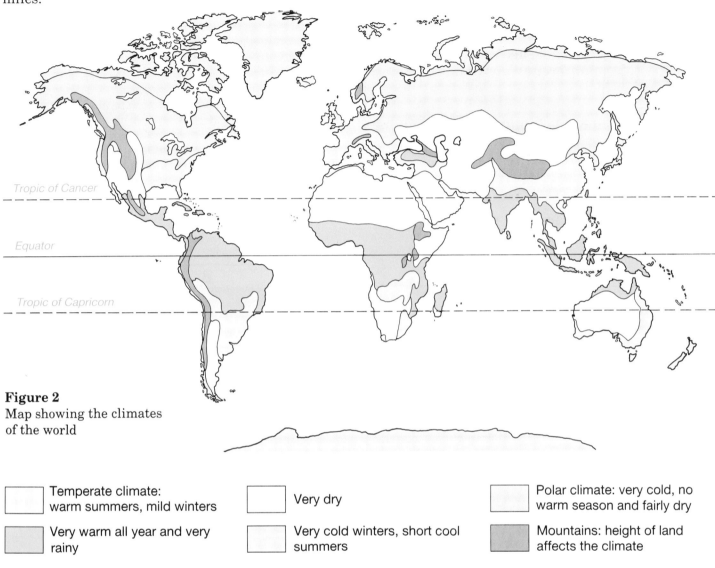

Figure 2
Map showing the climates of the world

	Temperate climate: warm summers, mild winters
	Very warm all year and very rainy
	Very dry
	Very cold winters, short cool summers
	Polar climate: very cold, no warm season and fairly dry
	Mountains: height of land affects the climate

M **Exercise C**

Match the words with their meanings.

Equator / Hemisphere / Capricorn / Cancer

1. _____ means one half of the world.
2. _____ is a line around the middle of the world.
3. _____ is the name of the northern tropic.
4. _____ is the name of the southern tropic.

Exercise D

List all the parts of the world which have a temperate climate. Describe them like this:

1. South-east Australia

Exercise E

On an outline map of the world, mark on all areas which have a temperate climate.

T **Exercise F**

Choose any one of the world's climates on the map, and describe its location.

Exercise G

1. Name any two continents shown on the map, and describe its location.
2. Describe the climates in the northern part of the two continents you have chosen.

Locating 1

Key words

symbols
grids

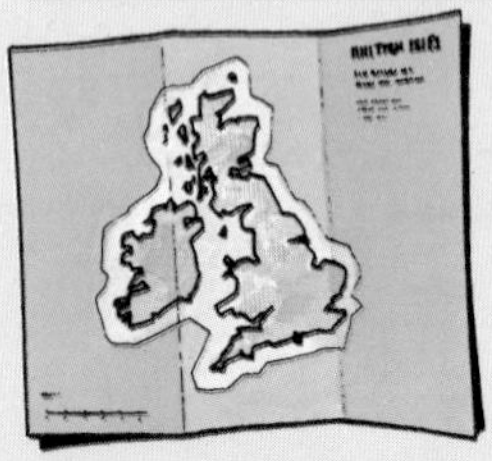

If you are lost or want to find out where a place is, use a map. This unit shows you different ways of finding places quickly.

This section is about locating places by naming the squares on a map.

Look at the symbols in the squares. The squares are called grids.

The school is in square C2.

Grids help us to find places on a map.

Look at this map of Treasure Island.

It shows some of the places on the island.

There is some treasure on the island.

Figure 1

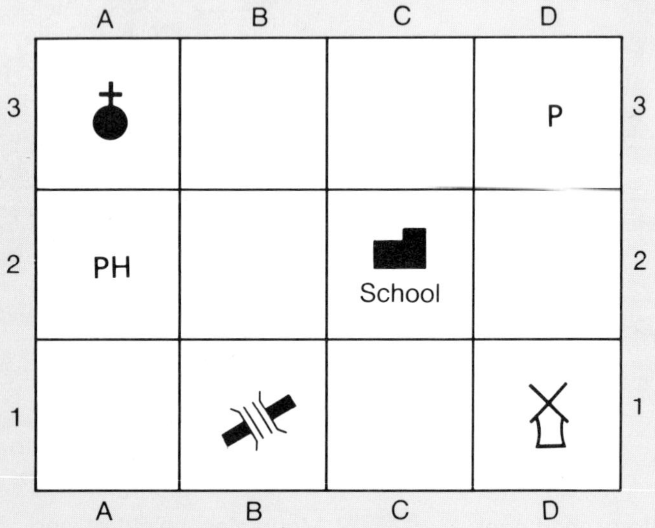

Figure 2 Treasure Island

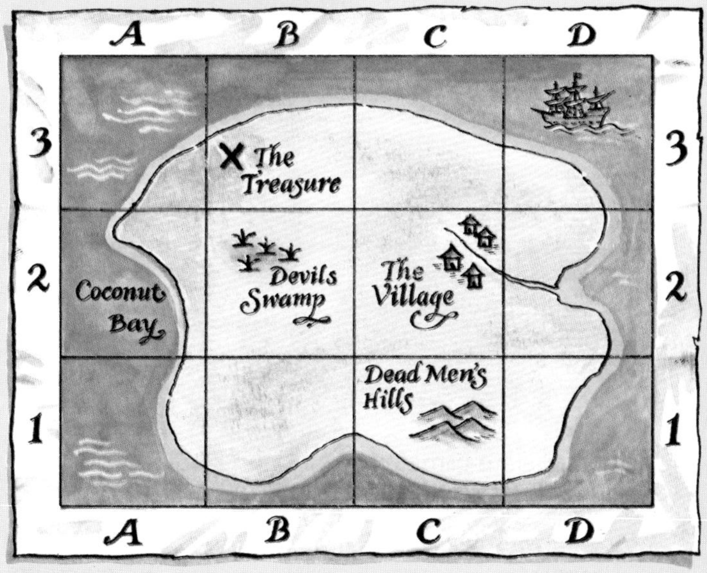

FS Exercise A

Look at Figure 1. Copy and complete these sentences. Like this:

1. The school is in square *C2* .
2. The church ( ) is in square ______ .
3. The bridge ( ) is in square ______ .
4. The post office (P) is in square ______ .
5. The windmill ( ) is in square ______ .
6. The public house (PH) is in square ______ .

Exercise C

Draw your own Treasure Island map. Make up names for five places. Draw a grid over your map, and label the grid.

FS Exercise B

Look at Figure 2. Locate the places on the map. Like this:

1. Devil's Swamp – *B2*
2. The Village –
3. Coconut Bay –
4. Dead Men's Hills –
5. The Treasure –

FS Exercise D

Copy and complete this sentence:

The treasure on my map is in square ______ .

Look at this map of a city centre:

Figure 3 Map of a city centre

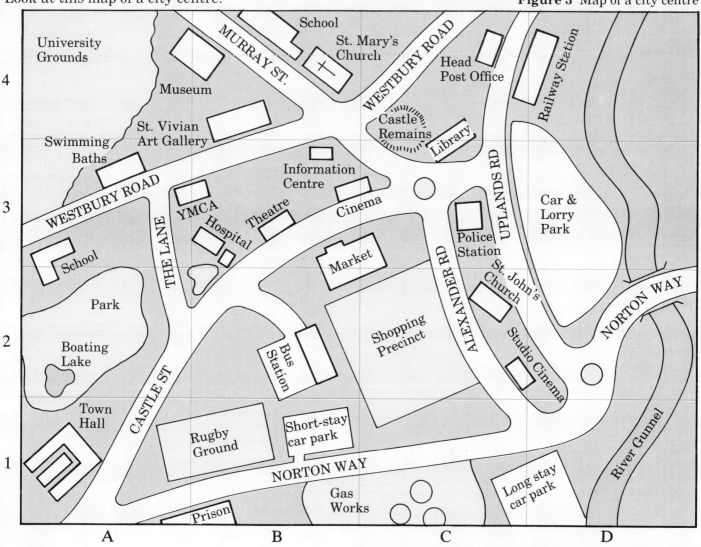

FG **Exercise E**

Look at the map and name the streets in these grid squares. Answer like this:

1. A3 = *Westbury Road* , *The Lane*
2. C4 = _____
3. B1 = _____
4. B3 = _____
5. C2 = _____

FG **Exercise G**

Give the grid squares for the following. Answer like this:

1. Boating Lake = *A2*
2. Car & Lorry Park = _____
3. Bus Station = _____
4. St. John's Church = _____
5. Police Station = _____
6. University Grounds = _____

FG **Exercise F**

Name the buildings found in these grid squares on the map:

1. A 3 _____   **4.** B3 _____
2. C4 _____   **5.** D4 _____
3. A1 _____   **6.** C2 _____

Exercise H

Use the map to plan a day in town, and describe where you would be at the following times. Like this:

9.00 a.m. = *Bus Station (B2)*
10.30 a.m. = _____
1.30 p.m. = _____
3.30 p.m. = _____
5.30 p.m. = _____

T **Exercise I**

Plan a day in your own town by using a local town map. Set out your day like Exercise H.

Locating 2

Key words

easting   grid reference
northing   National Park

This section is about locating places by naming the lines on a map.

On some maps, the lines and not the spaces have numbers. Look at this map of Bone Island.

Fish Lake is to the **east** of line 01.
Fish Lake is to the **north** of line 14.
Fish Lake is in square 0114.
This number is called a **grid reference**.

The lines 01 to 05 are called **eastings**, because you must look to the **east** of the line.
The lines 12 to 16 are called **northings**, because you must look to the **north** of the line.

The **first** two numbers of a grid reference are always the **eastings**.

Figure 1 Bone Island

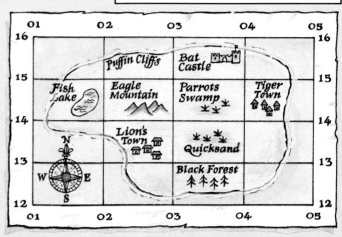

Figure 2
Cities in the British Isles

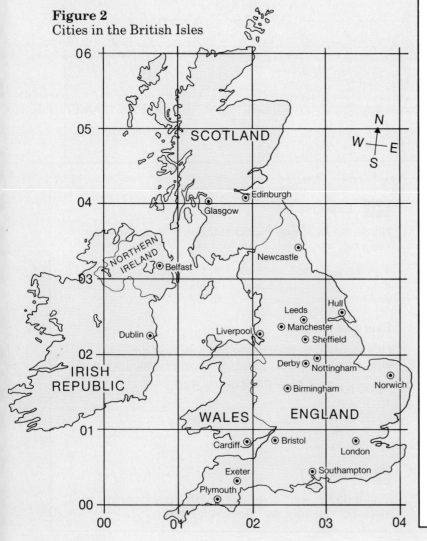

FG **Exercise A**

Look at Figure 1, the map of Bone Island. Write down what you will find at these grid references. Answer like this:

1. 0114 *Fish Lake*   **4.** 0312 _____
2. 0313 _____   **5.** 0214 _____
3. 0414 _____   **6.** 0314 _____

Exercise B

Give the grid references for these places:

1. Eagle Mountain   **3.** Puffin Cliffs
2. Bat Castle   **4.** Tiger Town

FG **Exercise C**

Look at Figure 2 and name the cities at these grid references. Answer like this:

1. 0300 *London*   **4.** 0003 _____
2. 0203 _____   **5.** 0002 _____
3. 0301 _____   **6.** 0302 _____

Exercise D

1. Name three cities east of easting 02.
2. Name three cities north of northing 03.

Exercise E

Give the grid references of your nearest city, and five others from Figure 2.

This map shows the National Parks in England and Wales. A National Park is an area of land where people can enjoy the beautiful landscape. They are often in highland areas, where there is not much industry.

Figure 3
National Parks of England and Wales

Photograph 1 Walking in the Yorkshire Dales National Park

Photograph 2 Rock-climbing in the Peak National Park

FG **Exercise F**

Look at Figure 3. Name the National Parks found at these grid references. Answer like this:

1. 0100 = *Dartmoor and Exmoor.*
2. 0202 = _____
3. 0102 = _____
4. 0101 = _____
5. 0203 = _____

Exercise G

Name your nearest National Park, and give its grid reference from Figure 3.

Exercise H

Look at the photographs above and describe what National Parks look like.

Exercise I

Write down five things you could do in a National Park, using the photographs to help you.

Exercise J

Choose one National Park and write about how you would spend a day there.

Locating 3

This section is about locating places by using map references.

Look at this map of Europe.
It is covered by a grid.

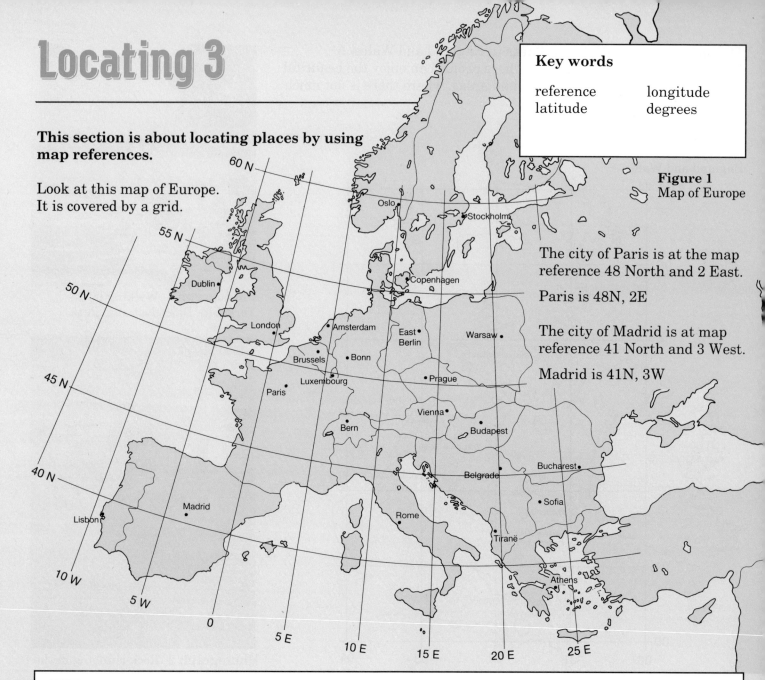

Figure 1
Map of Europe

The city of Paris is at the map reference 48 North and 2 East.

Paris is 48N, 2E

The city of Madrid is at map reference 41 North and 3 West.

Madrid is 41N, 3W

FG Exercise A

Name the cities you find located at these references.
Answer like this:

1. 42N, 12E = *Rome*
2. 53N, 6W = _____
3. 59N, 18E = _____
4. 49N, 6E = _____
5. 53N, 4E = _____
6. 51N, 4E = _____
7. 60N, 10E = _____
8. 39N, 9W = _____
9. 56N, 12E = _____
10. 51N, 7E = _____

FG Exercise B

Name the countries at these locations:

1. 39N, 4W = _____
2. 42N, 13E = _____
3. 47N, 3E = _____
4. 56N, 4W = _____
5. 53N, 8W = _____

Exercise C

Choose six cities not named in Exercise A and give the reference for each one.

On a map showing countries of the world, the lines going across are called lines of **latitude**. The lines up and down the map are called lines of **longitude**.

The lines are measured in **degrees**, and the sign for degrees is °. So the line of latitude called **forty-one degrees north** is written 41°N. The line of longitude called **three degrees west** is written 3°W, and so on.

So Madrid is really 41°N, 3°W. Paris is really 48°N, 2°E.

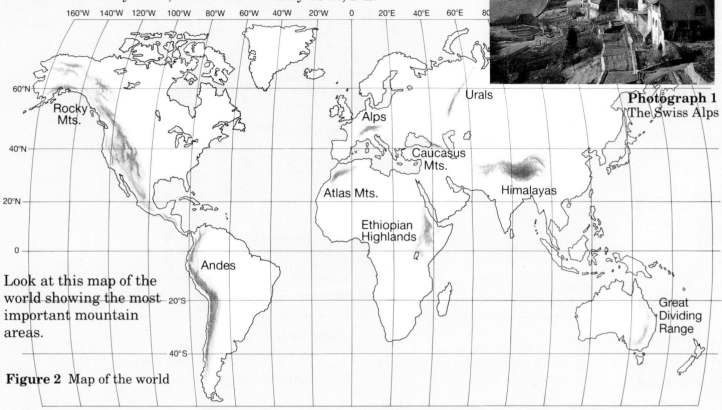

Photograph 1
The Swiss Alps

Look at this map of the world showing the most important mountain areas.

Figure 2 Map of the world

CH **Exercise D**

Look at the map of the world's mountains and copy and complete these sentences:

1. The mountains in Europe are called the (Alps / Andes).
2. The mountains in North America are called the (Andes / Rocky Mts.).
3. The mountains in South America are called the (Andes / Atlas Mts.).
4. The mountains in Asia are called the (Alps / Himalayas).
5. The mountains in Africa are called the (Atlas Mts. / Andes).

FG **Exercise E**

Name the mountains found at these map references. Answer like this:
1. 46°N   8°E = *The Alps*
2. 42°N 110°W = _____
3. 9°N   38°E = _____
4. 29°N   82°E = _____
5. 40°N   44°E = _____

Exercise F

Choose any three other mountain areas and give the map reference for each one.

Exercise G

Look at the photograph above. Imagine that you live in a mountain area. Write what you think it would be like to live there.

Locating 4

Key words

index
alphabetical

This section is about locating places in an atlas. An atlas is a book of maps.

An atlas has two parts: these are the maps and the **index**. The index is usually at the back of an atlas. It is a list of all the places, in alphabetical order.

The index also shows the latitude and longitude of a place, and the page number of the map in the atlas. Figure 1 shows part of a map index for the British Isles. Figure 2 shows part of a map index for the world.

A
Abercarn, Gwent	**13**	51N 3W
Aberdare, Mid Glamorgan	**13**	51N 3W
Aberdeen, Grampian	**16**	57N 2W
Abergavenny, Gwent	**13**	51N 3W
Abergele, Clwyd	**13**	53N 3W
Abertillery, Gwent	**13**	51N 3W
Aberystwyth, Dyfed	**13**	52N 4W
Abingdon, Oxfordshire	**12**	51N 1W
Accrington, Lancashire	**14**	53N 2W
Achill Island, Irish Republic	**17**	54N 10W

Figure 1
Index for British Isles

J
Jabalpur, India	**30**	23N 80E
Jackson, USA	**46**	32N 90W
Jacksonville, USA	**46**	30N 81W
Jaffna, Sri Lanka	**30**	9N 80E
Jaipur, India	**30**	27N 76E
Jakarta, Indonesia	**26**	6S 106E
JAMAICA, Caribbean	**47**	18N 77W
Jammu & Kashmir, Asia	**30**	34N 77E
Jamshedpur, India	**30**	23N 86E
JAPAN, Asia	**30**	36N 138E

Figure 2
Index for the world

Exercise A

Look at Figure 1, above. On which page will you find these places? Answer like this:

1. Aberdare − *page 13*
2. Abingdon −
3. Achill Island −
4. Aberdeen −
5. Abertillery −

Exercise B

Look at Figure 2, above. Give the latitude and longitude of these places. Answer like this:

1. Jaipur − *27N 76E*
2. Jacksonville −
3. Jamshedpur −
4. JAPAN −
5. Jaffna −

Exercise C

Copy these lists of countries and put them into alphabetical order:

1. Spain, Japan, USA, Argentina, India, Mexico, Brazil, Venezuela.
2. Italy, Canada, Iran, Colombia, Algeria, Argentina, Portugal, Poland.
3. Sudan, Senegal, Singapore, Syria, Sweden, Switzerland, Surinam.

Exercise D

Look at Figure 2, and name the countries where these places are located. Answer like this:

1. Jabalpur *is in India.*
2. Jakarta
3. Jaffna
4. Jamshedpur
5. Jackson

T Exercise F

Use the index in an atlas and give the latitude and longitude of ten world cities.

Exercise E

Write down the names of ten villages or towns in your county and put them in alphabetical order.

Look at this map of South America from the page of
an atlas. Figure 4 shows a part of the index in the atlas.

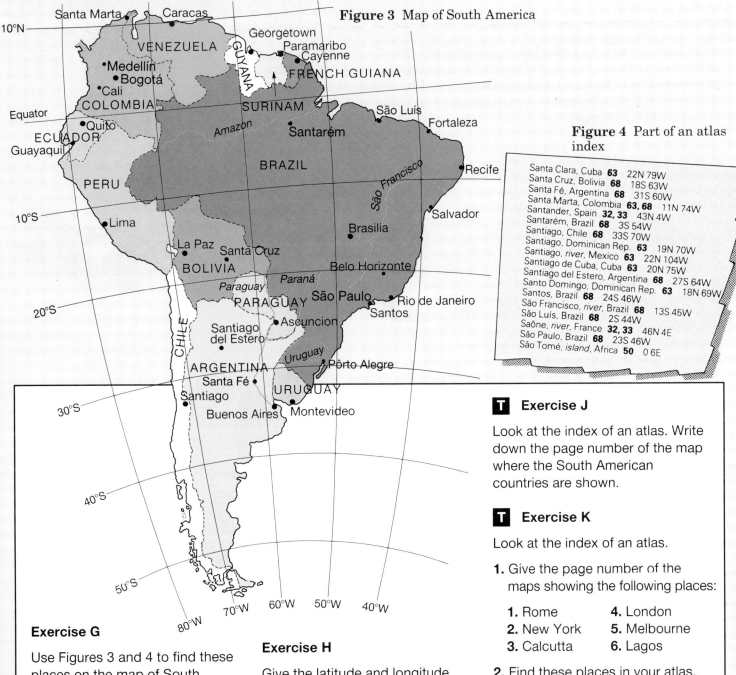

Figure 3 Map of South America

Figure 4 Part of an atlas index

Santa Clara, Cuba **63**   22N 79W
Santa Cruz, Bolivia **68**   18S 63W
Santa Fé, Argentina **68**   31S 60W
Santa Marta, Colombia **63, 68**   11N 74W
Santander, Spain **32, 33**   43N 4W
Santarém, Brazil **68**   3S 54W
Santiago, Chile **68**   33S 70W
Santiago, Dominican Rep. **63**   19N 70W
Santiago, *river*, Mexico **63**   22N 104W
Santiago de Cuba, Cuba **63**   20N 75W
Santiago del Estero, Argentina **68**   27S 64W
Santo Domingo, Dominican Rep. **63**   18N 69W
Santos, Brazil **68**   24S 46W
São Francisco, *river*, Brazil **68**   13S 45W
São Luís, Brazil **68**   2S 44W
Saône, *river*, France **32, 33**   46N 4E
São Paulo, Brazil **68**   23S 46W
São Tomé, *island*, Africa **50**   0 6E

Exercise G

Use Figures 3 and 4 to find these
places on the map of South
America, above.

1. Santa Fé
2. Santiago
3. Santos
4. São Francisco river
5. Santa Marta
6. Santarém
7. Santa Cruz
8. São Paulo

Exercise H

Give the latitude and longitude
of the places you located in
Exercise G. Answer like this:

1. Santa Fé = 31S 60W.

Exercise I

There are 13 countries in South
America. Use the map to find them
and write down their names in
alphabetical order.

T ## Exercise J

Look at the index of an atlas. Write
down the page number of the map
where the South American
countries are shown.

T ## Exercise K

Look at the index of an atlas.

1. Give the page number of the
   maps showing the following places:

   1. Rome   4. London
   2. New York   5. Melbourne
   3. Calcutta   6. Lagos

2. Find these places in your atlas,
   and for each one find and name
   the nearest ocean or sea.

Exercise L

Choose any letter from the
alphabet and give the latitude and
longitude of any **six** cities from
different countries beginning with
that letter.

Classification 1

This unit gives you practice in putting places and things into different groups. It will help you to understand how places are organized. At the end of this unit you will have a better understanding of a continent, a country, a state, a county, a city, a town and a village.

To start with, practise different ways of classifying animals. These animals are all found in the continent of North America:

1. wolf

2. buffalo

3. beaver

4. skunk

5. porcupine

6. caribou

7. walrus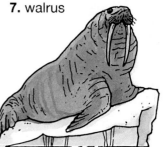

8. diamondback rattlesnake

Now look at this chart:

| | Animals | | | | | | | |
Groups	1	2	3	4	5	6	7	8
Animals with four legs.	✓	✓	✓	✓	✓	✓		
Animals with thick coats.	✓	✓	✓	✓				
Animals found only in North America.		✓		✓		✓		✓
Animals found in cold places.	✓		✓	✓		✓	✓	

Exercise A

Use the ticks in the chart above to write a sentence or two about each animal. Like this:

1. *A wolf has four legs, a thick coat, and is found in cold places. Wolves live in North America and in other countries.*

Exercise B

Make a chart like the one above, for six animals found in this country. Put the animals into four groups on your chart.

Look at these drawings of more animals found in North America.

9. moose

10. polar bear

11. seal

12. bald eagle

13. coyote

14. puma

15. alligator

16. jack rabbit

Exercise C

Copy and complete this chart. The first line has been done for you.

Groups	Animals							
	9	10	11	12	13	14	15	16
1. Animals found on land and in water.		✓	✓				✓	
2. Animals with thick coats.								
3. Animals with four legs.								
4. Animals that can fly.								
5. Animals that eat meat.								
6. Animals in the cat family.								
7. Animals found in cold places.								
8. Animals that do not eat meat.								

Exercise D

Look at all the animals with numbers from 1 to 16. Make your own chart for **all** the animals, like the one above.

Exercise E

Look at these three groups. Copy the boxes, and in them write as many names as you can.

People in my home	People in my street	People in my class

Classification 2

You can put places into groups, just as you did with animals on the pages before. Towns and cities may be located in a county, region or country. Countries may be grouped into continents. This section shows you ways of grouping and classifying places in North America.

North America is a large continent, and takes up about a fifth of the world's land surface. There are three major countries in North America: Canada, the United States of America (USA) and Mexico.

The northern part of Canada is very cold and covered by snow and ice for most of the year. But along the Gulf of Mexico it is so warm that they do not even have frost in winter.

Photograph 1
A view of northern Canada

Photograph 2 A swamp in southern USA

Figure 1 Map of North America

FG Exercise A

Look at Figure 1, and copy and complete these sentences:

1. The ocean to the east of North America is called the _____ Ocean.
2. The ocean to the west of North America is called the _____ Ocean.
3. The large bay to the north of Canada is called the _____ Bay.
4. The sea to the south of the United States of America is called the Gulf of _____ .

CH Exercise B

Copy and complete these sentences:

1. The northern part of Canada is very (hot / cold)
2. The southern part of the USA is very (hot / cold)

Exercise C

Write two sentences about each photograph to explain that they show different climates.

Figure 2 Map of North America showing cities

Figure 3 Map showing physical regions of Canada and the USA

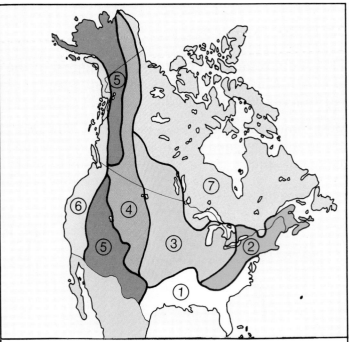

1. The Atlantic Plain   4. The Rocky Mountains
2. The Appalachian Mountains   5. The High Plateaux
3. The Central Lowlands   6. The Pacific Mountains
   7. The Canadian Shield

Exercise D

Look at Figure 2. Copy and complete these groups:

United States of America

Cities on the east coast   *New York*

Cities on the west coast

Cities on the south coast

Other cities

Canada

Cities west of Hudson Bay   *Winnipeg*

Cities east of Hudson Bay

Exercise E

Look at Figure 3 which shows physical regions of Canada and the USA. Copy and complete this chart. The first line has been done for you:

Groups	The Regions						
	①	②	③	④	⑤	⑥	⑦
1. Regions next to the Atlantic Ocean.	✓	✓					✓
2. Regions next to the Pacific Ocean.							
3. Regions only in the USA.							
4. Regions along the border with Mexico.							
5. Regions in both the USA and Canada.							
6. Regions next to the Great Lakes.							

Exercise F

Choose any three physical regions and name the cities in each region. Set out your answers in a chart.

Classification 3

Key words

provinces   tundra
territories   grasslands

This section looks at Canada, the biggest of the three countries of North America. It shows different ways of classifying the various regions of Canada.

Most Canadians live in towns and cities. This map shows the main towns and cities, and the ten provinces and two territories which make up Canada. Each province has its own government, which runs the schools, hospitals and other services. Few people live in the territories because it is so cold.

Key: Provinces and territories

1. British Columbia
2. Alberta
3. Saskatchewan
4. Manitoba
5. Ontario
6. Quebec
7. Newfoundland
8. Prince Edward Island
9. New Brunswick
10. Nova Scotia
11. Yukon Territory
12. North West Territories

Figure 1 Map of Canada showing provinces and cities

Exercise A

Look at the map showing cities and provinces in Canada. Name a city in each province, and set out your answers like this:

Province	**City**
British Columbia	Vancouver
Alberta	E......., C.......

Exercise B

Use the map to copy and complete this chart. The first line has been done for you.

		Provinces and territories											
Groups		1	2	3	4	5	6	7	8	9	10	11	12
1. Provinces and territories next to the Hudson Bay.					✓	✓	✓						✓
2. Next to the Atlantic Ocean.													
3. Next to the Great Lakes.													
4. Next to the USA border.													
5. Without a coastline.													

Outside the cities and towns are vast areas of forest, grassland and tundra. The grasslands are important for growing wheat. The forests are important for timber and in paper making.

Photograph 1 Vancouver

Photograph 2 The Rocky Mountains

Photograph 3 The tundra in northern Canada

Photograph 4 Wheat fields on the Canadian prairies

Exercise C

Copy and complete the chart:

Groups	Photographs			
	1	2	3	4
1. Photographs showing that Canada is a big country.				
2. Photographs showing that parts of Canada are very cold.				
3. Photographs showing that Canada has lots of open space.				
4. Photographs showing that much of Canada is forest.				
5. Photographs showing that Canada grows a lot of wheat.				
6. Photographs showing that Canada is different from Britain.				
7. Photographs showing that Canada is like Britain.				
8. Photographs showing that Canada has large cities.				

Photographs 1

This unit shows you how to look at photographs so you can get lots of information out of them.

Photograph 1 African forest

Photograph 2 Africa from space

Figure 1
Map of Africa showing climate

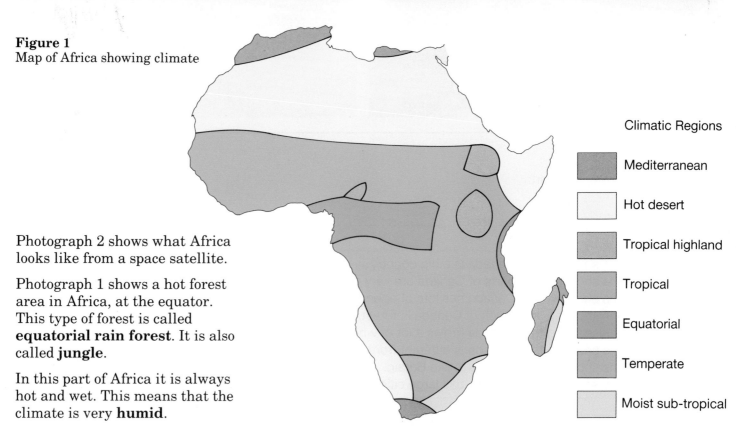

Climatic Regions

Mediterranean

Hot desert

Tropical highland

Tropical

Equatorial

Temperate

Moist sub-tropical

Photograph 2 shows what Africa looks like from a space satellite.

Photograph 1 shows a hot forest area in Africa, at the equator. This type of forest is called **equatorial rain forest**. It is also called **jungle**.

In this part of Africa it is always hot and wet. This means that the climate is very **humid**.

Plants and trees grow very quickly in the rain forest. There is no summer or winter at the equator.

It rains every day in the rain forest. The rain is very heavy.

If the plants and trees are cut down, the soil may be washed away by the heavy rain. This is called **soil erosion**.

This photograph shows an area of rain forest where the trees have been cut down. If the soil is washed away by the rain, nothing will grow there again. Large areas of rain forest have been lost in this way.

Photograph 3 An area of felled rain forest, Africa

Exercise A

All of these sentences about rain forests are true. Look at Photograph 1. Write down the sentences which you can **see** are true by looking at the photograph.

Plants and trees grow close together.
It is dark inside the rain forest.
It is hot in the rain forest.
There is very little wind in the jungle.
It is wet inside the rain forest.
Trees are very tall and straight.
All trees and plants are evergreens.
Trees have huge leaves at the top.
There are creepers hanging from some of the trees.
The rain forest has the same weather every day.

Exercise B

Explain how Photograph 1 shows that each of the sentences you chose from Exercise A is true.

Exercise C

Look at Photograph 3. Write down five things you can see in Photograph 3 that you cannot see in Photograph 1.

Exercise D

Write down three sentences to describe what the forest looks like after the trees have been cut down. (Use Photograph 3 to help you.)

Exercise E

Use a dictionary to find out what these words mean:

1. humid
2. dense
3. canopy
4. accessible
5. musty

Exercise F

Write five sentences about the rain forest. In each sentence include one of the words from Exercise E.

Photographs 2

This section uses photographs to look at deserts.

The driest places on earth are called deserts. They are very hot in the daytime, but cold at night. Plants and animals find it hard to survive. Deserts are lonely places. They are **deserted**.

Photograph 1 The desert in Saudi Arabia

Photograph 2 The desert in Utah, USA

CH   **Exercise A**

Look at the two different types of desert. Copy and complete these sentences:

Photograph 1 shows a (forest/desert) area in Saudi Arabia. It is a very (dry/wet) area and there are (many/few) plants.

Photograph 2 is a desert area in (Saudi Arabia/USA). The land is very (red/green). This means it is a (wet/dry) area.

Exercise B

Write down the things from the list below that you can see in **both** photographs:

red sand / yellow sand
mountains / camels / plants
rocks / roads / clouds

Exercise C

Write down the things from the list below that you cannot see in either photograph.

camels / people / clouds
cars / cities / rivers / plants
farms / buildings

Exercise D

1. Use a dictionary to find the meaning of these words:
   (a) survive, (b) deserted.
2. Write two sentences about the photographs above, including the words **survive** and **deserted**.

Some rivers, like the River Nile in the photograph below, flow through deserts. These rivers can be used on the dry soil, to water the land. This is called **irrigation**. The green areas in the photograph have been irrigated. It makes the land **fertile**.

In some parts of the deserts it may not rain for years. But there still may be water underground. If people can dig wells, this water can also be used to irrigate the land.

Plants help to hold the soil together and keep it from becoming too dry. But without rain, plants cannot grow. Dry soil becomes loose, like dust. The wind may blow the soil away. This is called **wind erosion**. If too many goats and other animals graze on the land, they eat up the plants, and then the dusty soil may blow away. People may cut down trees and bushes and this also causes wind erosion. Deserts made in these ways are man-made.

Photograph 3 The River Nile in Egypt

Photograph 4 The desert in Namibia, Africa

M **Exercise E**

Look at the photograph of the River Nile. Match the letters on the photograph with the words below:

> River Nile / mountains
> desert / irrigated land
> irrigation channels

M **Exercise F**

Look at Photograph 4. Match the letters on the photograph with the words below:

> village hut / fence
> grazing area / dusty land
> worn down path

M **Exercise G**

Match these words with their sentence endings:

> Irrigation / Fertile
> Wind erosion / Dust

1. _____ means rich soil.
2. _____ means watering the land.
3. _____ means wearing away the land.
4. _____ means dry soil.

Exercise H

1. Write two sentences to show how the deserts in Photographs 3 and 4 are alike.
2. Write two sentences to show how the deserts in Photographs 3 and 4 are different.

Exercise I

Choose one of the photographs and describe what you can see in the desert landscape.

page 31

Photographs 3

Key words

savanna   climates
season

This section uses photographs to look at hot grasslands in Africa.

Hot grasslands in Africa are between the tropical rain forests and deserts. The grasslands are called **savanna**.

This photograph shows the African savanna in the wet season:

Photograph 1

M   Exercise A

Match the letters on the photograph with the words below:

> rain clouds / giraffe / tall grass
> acacia tree / flat land

Exercise C

Write down three things you can see in the photograph which show it is the wet season.

CH   Exercise D

Copy and complete these sentences:

1. Hot grasslands are between the rainforests and (temperate / desert) areas.
2. In the photograph there are (many / no) mountains.

CH   Exercise B

Look at the photograph, and then copy and complete these sentences:

1. The grass is very (tall / short).
2. The land is very (brown / green) in the wet season.
3. The animals on the savanna plains include (cows / giraffes) and zebras.
4. The savanna has (few / many) trees.
5. Savanna areas are (hot / cold).

Exercise E

Describe in your own words what you can see in the photograph. (Write about six sentences.)

This photograph shows the African savanna in the dry season:

Photograph 2

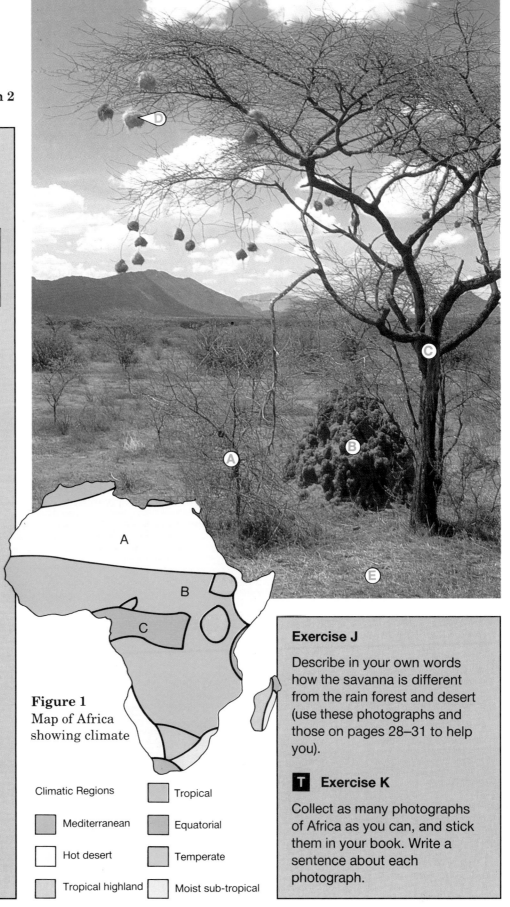

M **Exercise F**

Match the letters on the photograph with the words below:

> an acacia tree
> short brown grass
> thorn bush / termite mound
> weaver bird nest

T/F **Exercise G**

Look at the photograph of African savanna in the dry season, and write True or False for the sentences below. Answer like this: *1. True*

1. The photograph shows savanna in the dry season.
2. Most of the land is very brown.
3. The bushes do not have many leaves.
4. There are no clouds because it is the dry season.
5. The grass is very short.

Exercise H

Explain in your own words the differences between savanna lands in the wet and dry seasons. Use the photographs to help you.

CH **Exercise I**

Look at the map of Africa's climates, and complete the sentence below:

The photograph of the savanna was taken from position (A/B/C)

Figure 1
Map of Africa showing climate

Climatic Regions

☐ Mediterranean

☐ Hot desert

☐ Tropical highland

☐ Tropical

☐ Equatorial

☐ Temperate

☐ Moist sub-tropical

Exercise J

Describe in your own words how the savanna is different from the rain forest and desert (use these photographs and those on pages 28–31 to help you).

T **Exercise K**

Collect as many photographs of Africa as you can, and stick them in your book. Write a sentence about each photograph.

Photographs 4

This section uses photographs to look at some different scenes in Africa.

M **Exercise A**

Look at Photograph 1 and match the letters on the photograph with the words below:

> church / taxi / market
> bus stop / city centre

Exercise B

Look at Photograph 1 and name three things in the photograph that you can see in your city centre.

FG **Exercise C**

Look at Photograph 2 and then copy and complete the sentences below, using words from this list:

> season / savanna / grazing
> brown / cattle

Photograph 2 shows a village in the _____ lands of Africa. The land is very _____ , so this must be the dry _____ . There are some _____ near the river, where there is better _____ land.

Exercise D

In which photographs can you see these things? Write your answers like this:

	Photo 1	Photo 2	Both Photos
1. People	✓		
2. Cattle			
3. A river			
4. Trees			
5. Shops			
6. Homes			

Photograph 1 The city centre of Lagos in Nigeria

Photograph 2 A village on the Niger River in Niger

Exercise E

Name two things you can see in Photograph 2 that you might see near a village in Britain.

Exercise F

Explain how the scenes of Africa in Photographs 1 and 2 are very different from Britain.

M Exercise G

Look at Photograph 3, and match the letters on the photograph with the words in this list:

market / sand / palm tree
clear blue sky / flat-top house

Exercise H

Describe the clothes of the people in Photograph 3, and make a drawing of them.

T/F Exercise I

Look at Photograph 4, and write True or False for the sentences below:

1. There is a river in the photograph.
2. The vegetation is very green.
3. This is a wet part of Africa.
4. The trees are very tall.
5. There is a city in the photograph.
6. The trees are very close together.

Photograph 3 A village market in Mauritania

Photograph 4 The River Escravos in Nigeria

Exercise J

Look at the four photographs and copy and complete the chart below:

	Photograph 1	Photograph 2	Photograph 3	Photograph 4
1. A city	✓			
2. A village				
3. Savanna land				
4. Rain forest				
5. Desert				
6. A scene like Britain				
7. A scene different from Britain				

Sketches 1

Key words

Mediterranean
fruit

One of the best ways of making notes about a place is by drawing a sketch. This unit shows you how to draw different kinds of sketches.

This section uses sketches to look at the Mediterranean climate. The countries beside the Mediterranean Sea have summers that are hot and dry, with lots of sunshine. Most of the rain comes in the mild winters.

Look at the photograph and sketch of a Mediterranean coastal view.

Photograph 1 A Mediterranean coastal view

Figure 1 Sketch of Photograph 1

How to copy the sketch

Rule 1. Draw a box the same size as the sketch, like this:

Rule 2. Divide the box into quarters by drawing the lines from A to B, and C to D, like this:

Rule 3. Use the four boxes to guide you, and draw in the most important outlines. This sketch has been started for you.

Figure 2 How to draw a sketch

Exercise A

Copy and complete the sketch of Photograph 1.

The climate of the Mediterranean is the best in the world for growing citrus fruits, like oranges, grapefruits and lemons. It is also best for grapes, which are grown in vineyards. Look at this unfinished sketch of the vineyards shown in Photograph 2.

Photograph 2 Vineyards in Southern France

Figure 3 Unfinished sketch of Photograph 2

Photograph 3 Orange grove

Exercise B

Copy and complete the sketch of vines growing in Southern France.

Exercise C

Look at the photograph of the orange grove. Draw a sketch of the photograph. (Use the three rules on page 36 to help you.)

M Exercise D

Match the sketches of these fruits grown in Mediterranean climates, with words from the list: (Draw the sketches.)

grapes / orange / peach / lemon / grapefruit

Sketches 2

Key words

Mediterranean   Europe
Africa   holidays

This section gives you more practice in making sketches from photographs. Here the photographs are of seaside places in the Mediterranean region.

The map shows the countries which are on the shores of the Mediterranean Sea. Those on the south side are in Africa. Those on the north are in Europe.

The orange part of the map shows the areas which have a Mediterranean climate.

Figure 1 Map of the Mediterranean

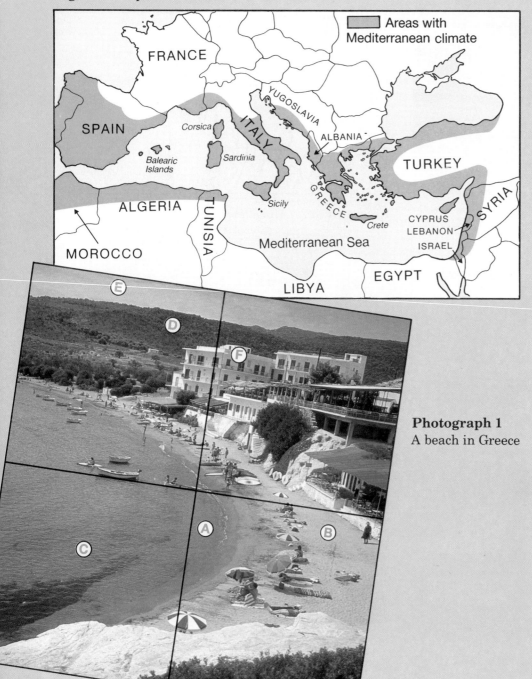

Photograph 1
A beach in Greece

Exercise A

Look at the map:

1. List the large islands in the Mediterranean sea.
2. List the countries with a Mediterranean climate.

M   Exercise B

Match the letters on the photograph with the words below:

   blue sky / bay / warm sea
sandy beach / hotel / rocky soil

Exercise C

Use the boxes on the photograph to draw a sketch of the beach scene. Draw it the same size as the photograph.

Exercise D

Label your sketch with the words from Exercise B.

Exercise E

1. Mediterranean areas are popular for holidays. Write down **five** things you can see in Photograph 1 which make Greece a popular place for holidays.
2. Write a sentence for each of the five things you have written down, explaining why you think they are important.

Photograph 2
A small harbour on one of the Greek Islands

Figure 2
Sketch of Photograph 2

Figure 3 Unfinished copy of Figure 2

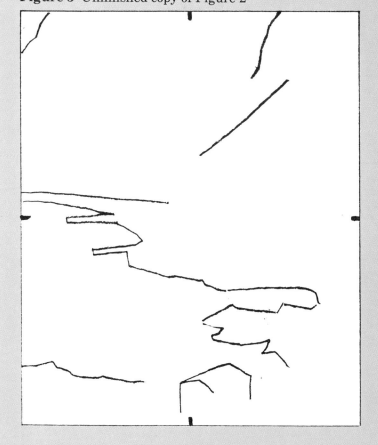

Exercise F

Look at Photograph 2 and Figure 2. Make up your own labels for the sketch at A−E. Answer like this:

A = warm calm sea

B =

Exercise G

Copy Figure 3, and complete the sketch. Use the four points on the box to guide you.

Exercise H

Label your sketch with your answers from Exercise F.

T **Exercise I**

Find some photographs of holiday places in a Mediterranean country and stick them into your book. Make a sketch of one of them.

Sketches 3

This section shows you how to sketch only part of a photograph.

The photographs on these pages are of California. There are several parts of the world where the summers are hot and dry and the winters not too cold. California has a climate like this, so we say it has a Mediterranean climate. Look at the map and see where in the world California is.

Figure 1 Map of the world showing Mediterranean climates

Look at this photograph of the city of San Francisco in California. It shows San Francisco Bay, and the Bay Bridge.

The sketches below show two parts of the photograph. Figure 2 shows the Bay Bridge. Figure 3 shows the city of San Francisco. Some parts of a photograph may show more information.

Photograph 1 San Francisco Bay

Exercise A

Look at Figure 1 and name the continents that have an area with a Mediterranean climate.

Exercise B

Look at Figure 2 and Figure 3. Decide which you think shows the more important part of the photograph, and then copy the sketch, making it the same size as it is on this page.

Exercise C

Label your sketch.

Exercise D

Give three reasons why you think your sketch shows the more important part of the photograph.

Exercise E

Write five sentences about what you can see in the photograph.

Figure 2 Sketch of the Bay Bridge

Figure 3 Sketch of the city of San Francisco

The Mediterranean areas in North America grow a lot of fruit. This photograph shows a fruit farm in California. The photograph has been divided into three parts.

Photograph 2 Fruit farm in California

Figure 4 Sketch of part of the fruit farm

 **Exercise F**

Match the parts of the photograph with the descriptions below:

Part 1 / Part 2 / Part 3

_____ shows a large field of orange trees, set out in long rows.
_____ shows a road for heavy traffic, and orange trees with tracks between them.
_____ shows a large flat area of fruit farms, with some mountains.

Exercise G

Look at the sketch (Figure 4) of Part 3 of the photograph.

1. Match the letters on the sketch with the words below:

    road / orange tree
    track

2. Write two sentences about Figure 4.

Exercise H

1. Draw a sketch of either Part 1 or Part 2 of the photograph.
2. Describe what you can see in your sketch.

Summarizing 1

Sometimes in geography you have to make notes. This unit shows you how to pick out useful information, and how to write it down.

This section is about choosing between different sentences.

This is Debs. She was asked by her English teacher to write about herself. This is what Debs wrote:

Some of the sentences in Debs' story tell us a lot about her. Some sentences tell us how she is the same as many other children. Others show how Debs is different from some other children.

> My name is Debra Angela Watson. My best friends call me Debs. I live at 17, Filbert Road Middleton with my Mum and my brother Alan. In the holidays I stay with my Dad. I like watching television and listening to records. I am 13 years old, and my birthday is on April 23rd. I go to Middleton Comprehensive School. I get up at 7.30 every morning and help my Mum to make the breakfast. I get Alan ready for school. I always brush my teeth and wash in the mornings. My favourite food is chips and my favourite lesson is drama.

Exercise A

Read Debs' story again.

1. Copy any two of the sentences that show Debs is like most girls her age.
2. Copy any sentences that may only be true about Debs.

FG Exercise B

Look at this form. Copy and complete the form for Debs. She has already started it.

Exercise C

Copy out this form again, but fill it in about yourself.

Exercise D

Write a story about yourself. Write five sentences that show you are like most children of your age. Write five sentences that are true only about you.

Surname	_Watson_
Christian or Forenames	_Debra Angela_
Age	_____years
Address	_____
	_____
	_____
Name of school	

Look at this map. It shows Debs' home town of Middleton. It has many of the things that lots of other places have. But there are also things about Middleton that are different. All places have something special about them, when you look at them closely.

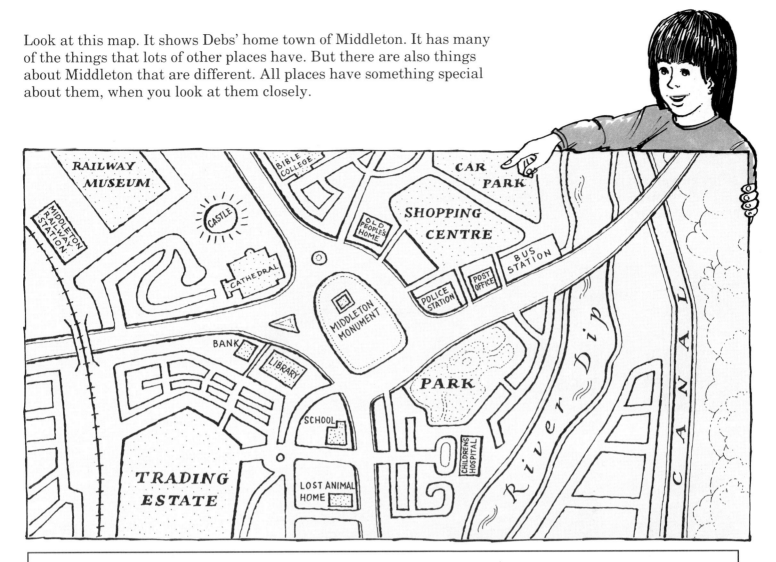

Exercise E

If you think a sentence below shows that Middleton is like many towns write SAME. If it does not, write DIFFERENT. Answer like this: *1. same*

1. Middleton has traffic lights.
2. Middleton has shops.
3. Middleton is an old Roman town.
4. Middleton is beside a river.
5. Middleton has a camera factory.
6. Middleton is busy on Saturday.
7. Middleton is the birthplace of a famous writer called Tom Benson.
8. Middleton's shops are in the centre of town.

Exercise F

Copy out the sentences from Exercise E for which you wrote DIFFERENT.

Exercise G

Look at the map:

1. Write down **five** buildings in Middleton that are also in your home town.
2. Write down **five** buildings in Middleton that are not in your home town.
3. Write down **five** buildings in your home town that are not shown on the map of Middleton.

Exercise H

1. Write down **eight** sentences about your home town.
2. Underline in red the sentences that show your home town is different from many other towns.

T Exercise I

Find out from your library all you can about your home town. Write a letter to a friend describing your town.

Summarizing 2

This section shows you how to make notes or summaries from photographs.

Maps and photographs can show a lot of information. Only some of this information may help you to answer a question. You will have to choose the most relevant information. Then you can write it down.

LOOK   CHOOSE   WRITE

Photograph 1 Valley of the River Dip

A geography class have been asked to look at this photograph of the River Dip, near Middleton. They have to write about how the land is used in this part of the valley.

T/F **Exercise A**

Look at the photograph and write True or False.

1. Most of the land is grassland.
2. There are trees on the valley sides.
3. This is farmland.
4. There are some sheep in the valley.
5. The valley bottom is wet.
6. There are no farm buildings.
7. There is a tractor in the fields.
8. There are no cows in the fields.
9. The valley is shaped like the letter V.
10. The fields are big.

Exercise B

Choose the most useful true sentences from Exercise A, like this. If the sentence gives correct information about how the land is used write YES. If it does not, write NO.
Answer like this: *1. Yes*

Exercise C

Write down all the sentences in full, from Exercise B, to which you gave a YES answer.

page 44

A **summary** is a short piece of writing that has only relevant information. Writing down relevant information is called **summarizing**.

Look at this photograph of a valley in the Alps in Switzerland.

Photograph 2
Valley in the Swiss Alps

M **Exercise D**

Look at Photograph 2. Match the letters on the photograph with the words below:

steep valley sides
road / farm building
woods on high slopes
valley floor

T/F **Exercise E**

Look at Photograph 2 and write True or False for these sentences.

1. The valley sides are very steep.
2. There is very little flat land.
3. The farms are very big.
4. There is a road along the valley floor.
5. This valley is shaped like the letter U.

Exercise F

Here are four summaries of Photograph 2.

1. **Choose** the best summary, and copy and complete this sentence: The best summary is (summary 1/2/3/4).
2. Say what is wrong with the other summaries.

Summary 1
This valley has steep sides and lots of farms. There is a road in it, and some trees. The trees are high up, but the grass is not.

Summary 2
This valley is not in Britain. The farms are small, and so are the woods. There is a road in the valley.

Summary 3
This valley is U-shaped. It is steep, with small farms, grassland and woods. It is in a different country.

Summary 4
This U-shaped valley in the Swiss Alps has woodland on the higher slopes and grass lower down. The small farms on the valley floor are close to the main road.

Exercise G

Write down the best summary.

Summarizing 3

This section is about key words and key sentences.

Here are some of the ways the earth's water is stored:

Figure 1

Figure 2

Figure 3

Figure 4

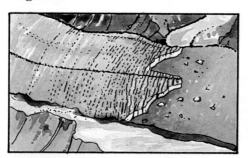

Figure 5

Figure 6

Figure 7

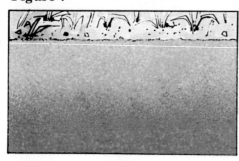

Figure 8

Figure 9

M **Exercise A**

Match the sketches above with the words below.
Answer like this: *1. Figure 1 = river*

lake / river / iceberg
atmosphere / glacier / ocean
spring / stream / soil and groundwater

FG **Exercise B**

Complete the sentences below, using some of the
words from Exercise A. Answer like this:

1. A *river* is a large stream of water.
2. A _____ is a slow-moving river of ice.
3. The _____ is the air around us.
4. An _____ is a large sea.
5. A _____ is where underground water comes to the
surface.

Words that help to explain anything that is difficult and important are called **key words**. Sentences with key words in them are **key sentences**. These can help you to write a summary.

Look at this diagram and read the text below:

Figure 10 The water cycle

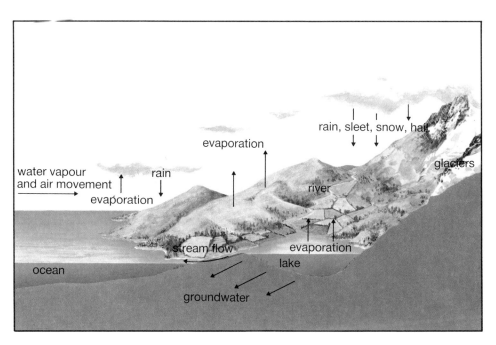

Most of the earth's water is found in oceans, rivers and lakes. In cold places it is found as slow-moving rivers of ice called glaciers. But water is also found in the air. Water in the form of tiny droplets or vapour is in the atmosphere. When water is taken into the atmosphere, this is called evaporation. Water that falls from the atmosphere as rain, sleet, snow or hail, is called precipitation.

Exercise C

The words in the list below were all used in the text. Choose and write down the key words.

> called / oceans / it / glaciers / vapour / the / found / most
> precipitation / atmosphere / evaporation / as / in

Exercise D

Write a sentence for each of the key words you chose in Exercise C.

Exercise E

Copy the summary and drawings below, but in the right order.

Water runs into streams, rivers, or into the ground.

Water evaporates into the air.

Streams and rivers run into the sea.

Rain, sleet or snow falls from the sky.

Water vapour is carried by the wind.

Exercise F

Write down the names of places near your home where water is found, and describe if they are rivers, streams, lakes or something else.

Summarizing 4

This section is about making comparisons.

Look at this photograph of the area near the North Pole:

Photograph 1 A polar bear in the Arctic

The area near the North Pole is called the Arctic. In winter, the sun is not very strong because it is very low in the sky. At the North Pole, the dark, cold winters last for about six months. In summer, the sun does not set, and there are six months of daylight.

The sea at the North Pole is covered by thick ice. The largest animal on the ice is the polar bear. It is only found in the Arctic. Other large animals found in the Arctic Ocean include whales, seals and walruses.

M   **Exercise A**

Match the letters on the photograph with the words below:

ice / polar bear / sea

Exercise B

1. Choose four key words from the text about the North Pole. Write them down.
2. Use your key words to write a summary of the North Pole, from the text.

T   **Exercise C**

Find out all you can about the North Pole from a library or an encyclopaedia. Write ten important sentences about it.

Look at this photograph of the area near the South Pole:

Photograph 2 Penguins in Antarctica

Exercise D

Look at Photographs 1 and 2.

1. Write two sentences to show how the photographs are similar.
2. Write two sentences to show how the photographs are different.

Exercise E

Are these sentences about **Antarctica**, the **Arctic**, or **both**. Answer like this: *1. Both*

1. It is a very cold place.
2. Polar bears are found there.
3. Mountains are found there.
4. Penguins live there.
5. It has a very long, cold, dark winter.
6. It has a very long summer, with lots of daylight.
7. It has very thick ice.
8. Icebergs are found there.
9. Whales swim in these oceans.
10. Mid-summer is in December.

Exercise F

Use your answers from Exercise E to write a summary called **The Polar Lands**.

Unlike the Arctic, the area around the South Pole is a frozen continent, and not just a frozen ocean. The continent is called Antarctica. Most of the land is covered by very thick ice. At the edge of the area covered by ice, blocks of ice break off to form icebergs. These drift out into the ocean.

The Antarctic is like the Arctic in some ways. The South Pole also has long summer days, when the sun never sets, and long winter nights when the sun never rises. But when it is winter at the North Pole, it is summer at the South Pole. Antarctica has its mid-summer in December.

Animals found at the Antarctic include whales, seals and squid. There are many birds, and perhaps the most famous of all are penguins. These birds are not found in the Arctic.

Map Drawing 1

Key words

accurately
grid

There will be many times when you have to draw a map: to show a friend where a place is, or to make a summary for example. This unit shows you how to draw different types of maps.

A drawing can be copied accurately if it is covered by a grid. Look at this drawing:

Figure 1 Drawing of Sydney Opera House and the Harbour Bridge

The drawing is covered by eight squares. In each square there is a part of the drawing.

The drawing can be copied accurately if it is copied one square at a time.

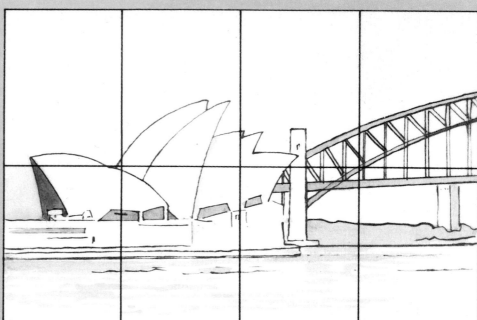

Some of the squares have been copied on to this grid. They show only a part of the drawing. If the other squares are copied in this way, the drawing can be finished.

Figure 2 Unfinished drawing of Sydney Opera House and the Harbour Bridge

Exercise A

1. Draw a grid the same size as in Figure 1.
2. Use your grid to copy Figure 2.
3. Complete the drawing.

Exercise B

1. Cut out a drawing from a newspaper or magazine.
2. Stick it into your book.
3. Cover the drawing with a grid, and make a copy of it.

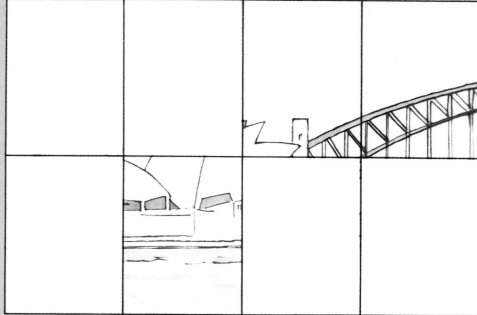

Look at this outline map of Australia. It can be copied accurately by using the grid as a guideline.

Figure 3 Outline map of Australia

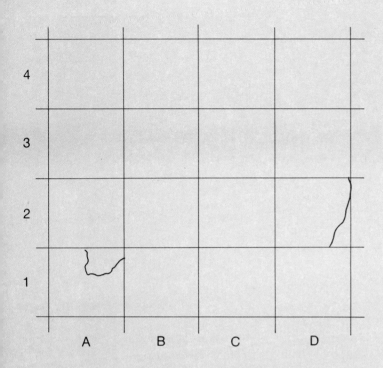

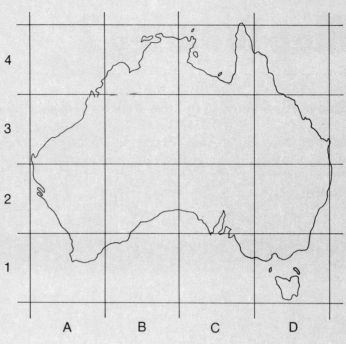

Figure 4 Outline map started

This map of Australia has been started. The shapes in A1 and D2 have been drawn in.

Figure 5 Map of Australia showing cities

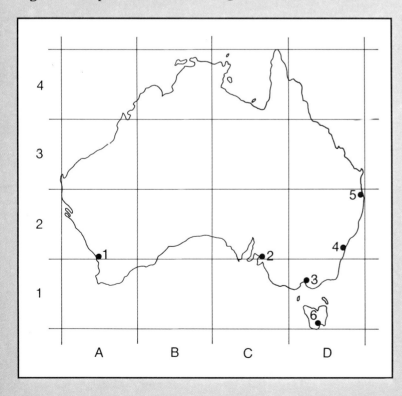

Exercise C

1. Copy the grid from Figure 3.
2. Copy A1 and D2 on to your grids.
3. Complete the map of Australia on your grids.

Exercise D

Use Figure 5 to mark the cities of Australia on to your map.

Exercise E

Use an atlas to name the cities on your map. Answer like this:

1 = Perth

Map Drawing 2

Key words

Australia   states
outline

This section shows you how to draw a sketch map.

Look at this map of Australia. Some of the points on the
shape of Australia have been marked by dots.

Figure 1

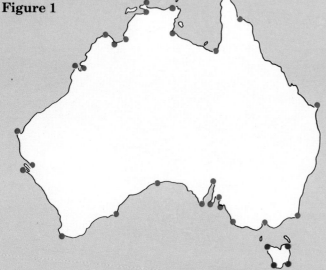

Figure 2

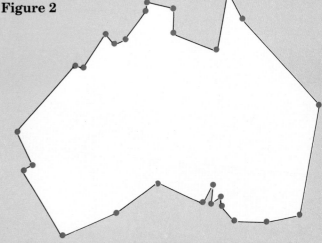

On this map, the points on the outline
shape of Australia have been joined together.

This map does not show the exact shape of
Australia. It is called a **sketch map**.
Sketch maps are quick and simple ways of
drawing maps.

Exercise A

Look at Figure 3.

1. Copy the pattern of dots,
using the grids to help you.
2. Join the dots on your map to
draw a sketch map of
Australia.

Exercise B

1. Place a sheet of tracing
paper over any map in an
atlas.
2. Mark dots on to the tracing
paper to show its shape.
3. Copy the pattern of dots and
join them together to draw a
sketch map.

Figure 3

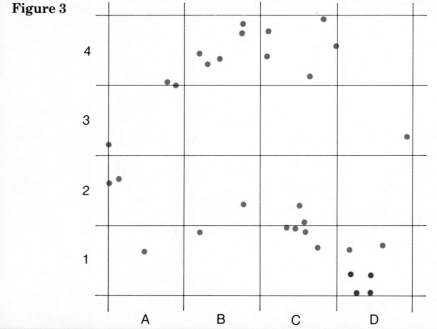

A sketch map can be labelled, to show more information.

This sketch map shows the seven states of Australia.

Figure 4

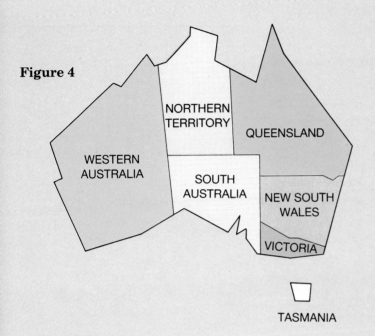

This sketch map shows Australia's wet and dry areas.

Figure 5

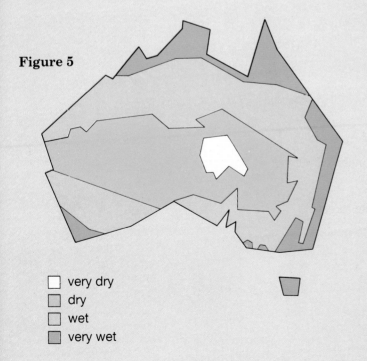

- ☐ very dry
- ☐ dry
- ☐ wet
- ■ very wet

Exercise C

Draw one sketch map of Australia, showing the states and the wet and dry areas.

M **Exercise D**

Match these continents with their sketch maps, and draw the sketch maps each time:

Africa / South America
North America

Exercise E

1. Copy this pattern of dots, using the grid to help you (Figure 7). Do not copy the numbers.
2. Join the dots in the correct order.
3. Name the country which the sketch map shows. (Use an atlas.)

Figure 6

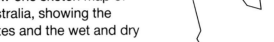
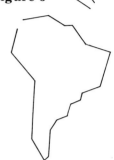

Figure 7

Map Drawing 3

Key words

regions
location

This section gives you more practice in drawing sketch maps and sketches of photographs.

Look at this sketch map of Australia. It divides the country into a number of regions.

The photographs come from four of the regions shown on the map. The location of Photograph 1 is shown by a line joining it to the sketch map.

Photograph 1

Photograph 2

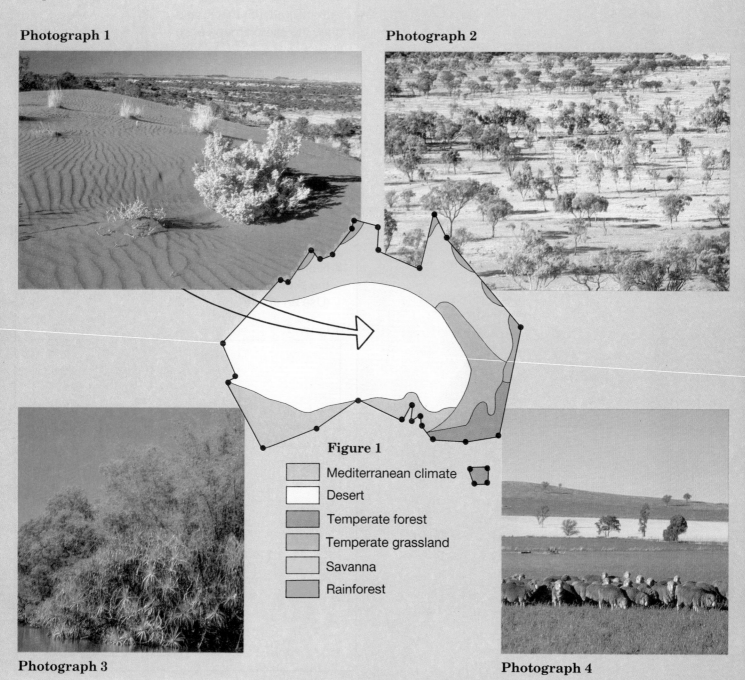

Figure 1

- Mediterranean climate
- Desert
- Temperate forest
- Temperate grassland
- Savanna
- Rainforest

Photograph 3

Photograph 4

Exercise A

Copy the sketch map of Australia, and draw sketches of the photographs. Make them the same size as those on page 54, and set them out like this:

M Exercise B

Match the photographs on page 54 with the summaries below:

Photograph 1 / Photograph 2
Photograph 3 / Photograph 4

_____ is an area of tropical vegetation, beside a river. It is in the Northern Territory, and shows bamboo and mangrove vegetation.

_____ is an area of grassland. It shows part of a large sheep farm in New South Wales.

_____ is an area of desert. It is south of Alice Springs, in the Northern Territory and shows a sand dune and vegetation.

_____ is an area of savanna vegetation, in Queensland. It shows dry, flat country and scattered trees. It is near mountains called the Selwyn Range.

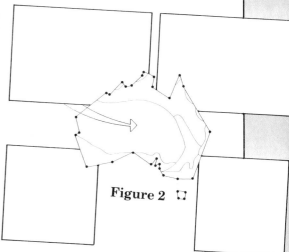

Figure 2

Exercise C

Join your sketches to your sketch map of Australia, like Photograph 1 on page 54.

Exercise D

1. Look at the photograph of the city of Sydney, in Australia. Match the letters on the photograph with the words below.

Sydney Harbour / Sydney Bridge
Sydney Opera House

2. Write down three ways that Sydney is like cities in this country.
3. What do you think are some of the problems of living in a city like Sydney?

Photograph 5 Sydney

Scale 1

Key words

size   scale
shape

Maps come in different sizes, for different reasons. This unit gives you practice in dealing with maps of different sizes.

This is Tom.

This is Tom standing nearer.

This is Tom standing further away.

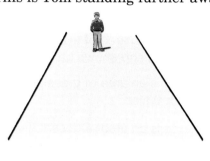

In the pictures, Tom's size looks as if it has been changed. But really, Tom is only one size. He just looks different when he moves.

Exercise A

In each of the sets of pictures below, all the objects are really the same size. But one is near and one is far away. Draw and label the ones that are near and far. Like this:

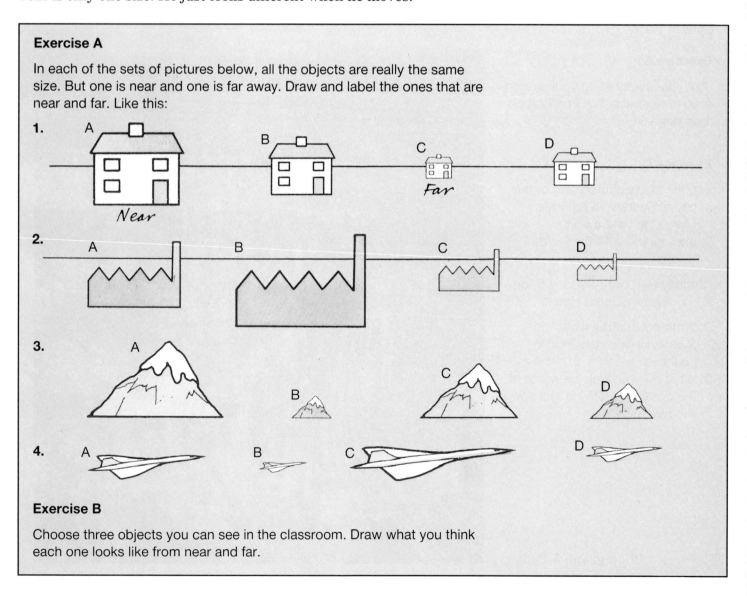

1. A   B   C   *Far*   D
Near

2. A   B   C   D

3. A   B   C   D

4. A   B   C   D

Exercise B

Choose three objects you can see in the classroom. Draw what you think each one looks like from near and far.

Look at this plan of a room. The room is really forty times bigger than it is on this page. But its shape is the same as it is on the plan.

The link between the size of an object and its shape is called **scale**.

So the scale of this plan is 1:40.

Figure 1 Plan of a room

M **Exercise C**

Look at the plan, and match the letters with the words in this list:
Answer like this: *A = door*

> table / door / carpet
> chair / wardrobe / bed

Exercise D

Make an accurate copy of the plan so it has the same scale as Figure 1, like this:

1. Draw a box the same size as the plan.
2. Draw in the line from L to R (very lightly) so it is in the same place on your copy.
3. Do the same for the line from T to B.
4. Use the lines L−R, and T−B as guide lines to draw the plans for the table, door, carpet, chair, wardrobe and bed.

Exercise E

Look at the plan below. It shows the same room, but it has a different scale. Copy and complete the plan. (Start by drawing the shape of the room.)

Figure 2

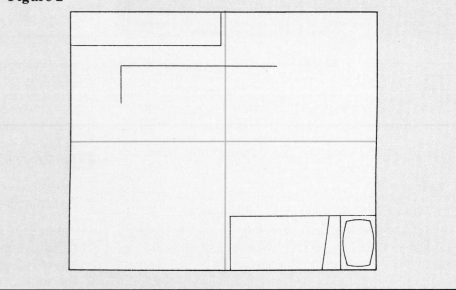

Scale 2

Key words

photograph   reduced
grid pattern   cemetery

This section shows how you can change the scale of a map and draw the same map to different sizes.

Look at the photograph and map below. They show the same area. Everything shown on the photograph and the map has been reduced 1500 times. So the scale of the photograph and the map is 1:1500.

Photograph 1 Aerial photograph of part of a village

Figure 1 Map of the same area

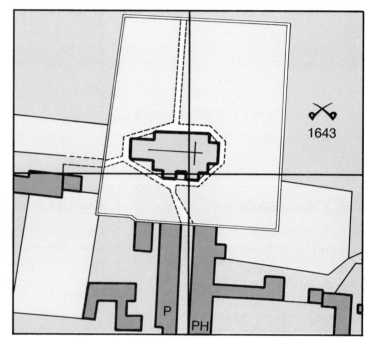

M **Exercise A**

Look at the photograph and match the letters with the words below:

    houses / church / path / road / churchyard

Exercise B

1. Write down two things you can see in the photograph that are not on the map.
2. Write down two things you can see on the map, that are not in the photograph.

Exercise C

Look at the map and draw the symbols that are used to show the houses, the church, the path, the road and the battlefield.

Exercise D

Look at the reduced map (Figure 2). Use the grids as a guide to copy and complete the map.

CH **Exercise E**

Copy and complete these sentences:

1. Figure 2 is (half / twice) the size of Figure 1.
2. The scale of Figure 2 is (1:750 / 1:3000).

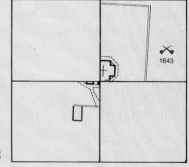

Figure 2

The scale of a map can be changed by using the grids.

Look at this map of Great Britain. Its scale is 1:13 000 000.

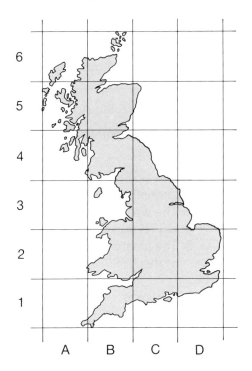

Figure 3 Map of Great Britain

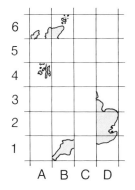

Figure 4 Grid pattern

This is the same grid pattern, but the grids are a different size. These grids are half the size. So the scale of this map is 1:26 000 000.

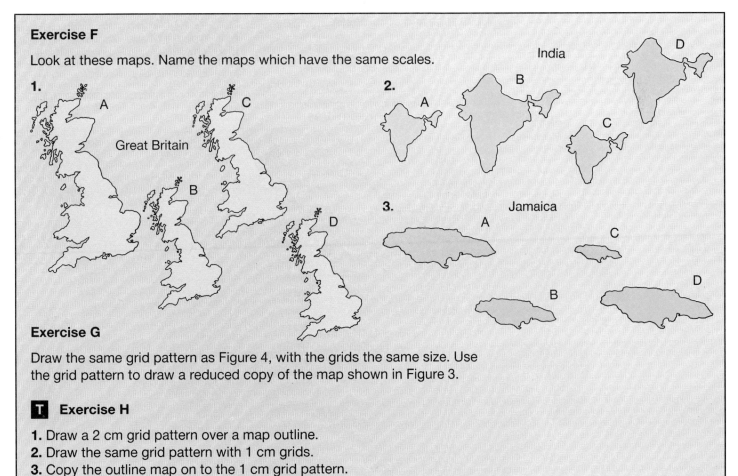

Exercise F

Look at these maps. Name the maps which have the same scales.

1. Great Britain

2. India

3. Jamaica

Exercise G

Draw the same grid pattern as Figure 4, with the grids the same size. Use the grid pattern to draw a reduced copy of the map shown in Figure 3.

T **Exercise H**

1. Draw a 2 cm grid pattern over a map outline.
2. Draw the same grid pattern with 1 cm grids.
3. Copy the outline map on to the 1 cm grid pattern.

Scale 3

This section shows how map makers use scale to show the size of a very large country.

The largest country in the world is the USSR. It has one-seventh of all the world's land. The western part is in Europe, but the eastern part is in Asia.

USSR are the initial letters of the Union of Soviet Socialist Republics. This is the proper name of the country we call the Soviet Union or sometimes just Russia.

The distances between some of the cities are very large. The Trans-Siberian Railway from Moscow to Vladivostok is the longest in the world.

This is a map of the USSR. The scale of the map is 1:50 000 000. This means that 1 cm on the map equals 500 km on the ground.

Figure 1
Map of the USSR

CH **Exercise A**

Copy and complete these sentences:

1. The USSR is the (smallest / largest) country in the world.
2. The western part of the USSR is in (Europe / Asia).
3. The (eastern / western) part of the USSR is in Asia.

Exercise B

1. Draw the outline of the USSR on tracing paper.
2. Trace the outline of Britain from Figure 1 as many times as you can, inside your tracing of the USSR.
3. How many times bigger than Britain is the USSR?

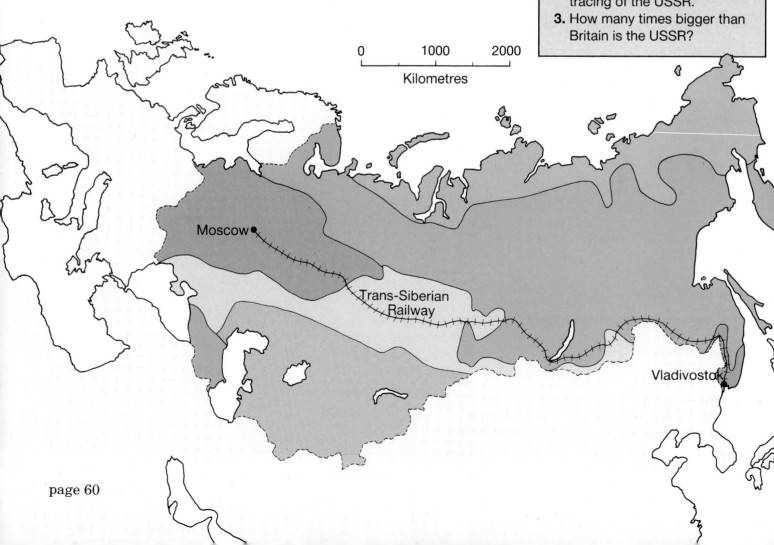

Tundra　　　Mixed forest
Grassland　　Coniferous forest
Steppe and semi-desert

0   1000   2000
Kilometres

Moscow●

Trans-Siberian
Railway

Vladivostok

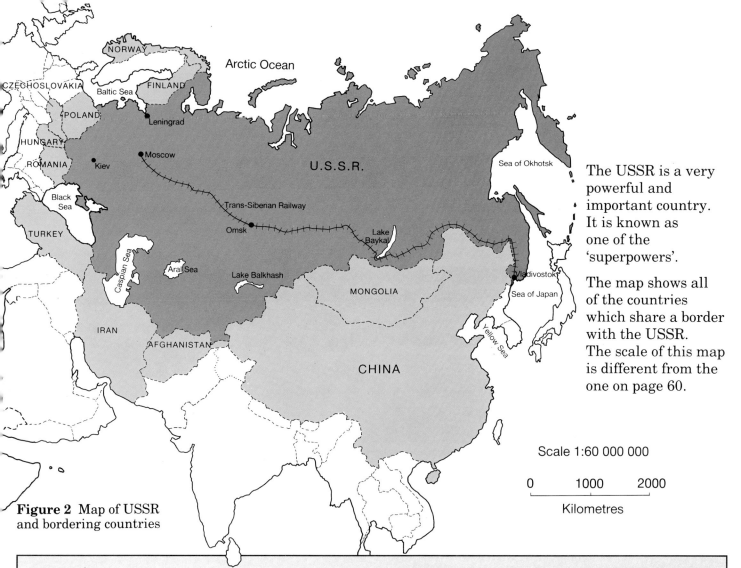

The USSR is a very powerful and important country. It is known as one of the 'superpowers'.

The map shows all of the countries which share a border with the USSR. The scale of this map is different from the one on page 60.

Scale 1:60 000 000

0   1000   2000
Kilometres

Figure 2 Map of USSR and bordering countries

Exercise C

Look at the two maps of the USSR.

1. What are the scales of the maps?
2. What is the main difference between the size of these maps?

Exercise D

Look at the map above. Name five countries which share a border with the USSR.

FG Exercise E

Look at Figure 1, and use your tracing to complete these sentences:

1. The area of tundra in the USSR is about _____ times the size of Britain.
2. The area of coniferous forest in the USSR is about _____ times the size of Britain.
3. The area of steppe and semi-desert in the USSR is about _____ times the size of Britain.

Exercise F

Look at Figure 2.

1. Name a country which is about the same size as Britain.
2. Name a country which is about twice the size of Britain.

Exercise G

Choose any country shown on the map above (but *not* the USSR). Compare the size of the country you have chosen with the size of the USSR and Britain. (You may use tracing paper to help you.)

T Exercise H

Collect some photographs of the USSR from magazines and stick them into your book. Describe what the photographs show.

Scale 4

This section uses scale to look at the size and geography of the USA.

The United States of America, called USA for short, is the second largest country in the continent of North America. The USA is divided into 50 large areas. Each area is called a **state**, and 48 of the states are in one block. The other two states are Hawaii, which is in the Pacific Ocean, and Alaska which is north-west of Canada.

The USA is a rich and powerful country. It is also called a 'superpower' like the USSR. Look at this map of the states of the USA.

Figure 1 Map of USA

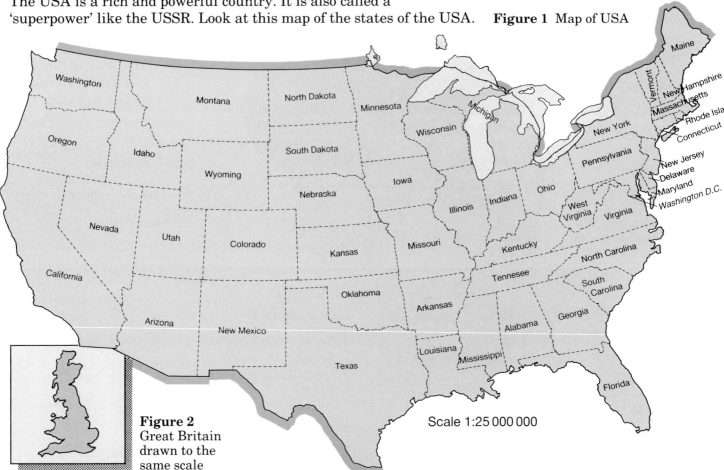

Scale 1:25 000 000

Figure 2
Great Britain
drawn to the
same scale

Exercise A

Look at the map of the USA. What is the scale of the map?

Exercise B

1. Name the largest state shown on the map.
2. Name the smallest state.

Exercise C

Name five states in the USA which are about the same size as Britain.

Exercise D

Name any states which are much bigger than Britain.

This is the state of Texas taken from the map:

Figure 3

Figure 3 and Figure 4 have the same scales.

This is the state of Florida taken from the same map:

Figure 4 Florida

This is the state of Florida drawn at a different scale:

Figure 5 Florida

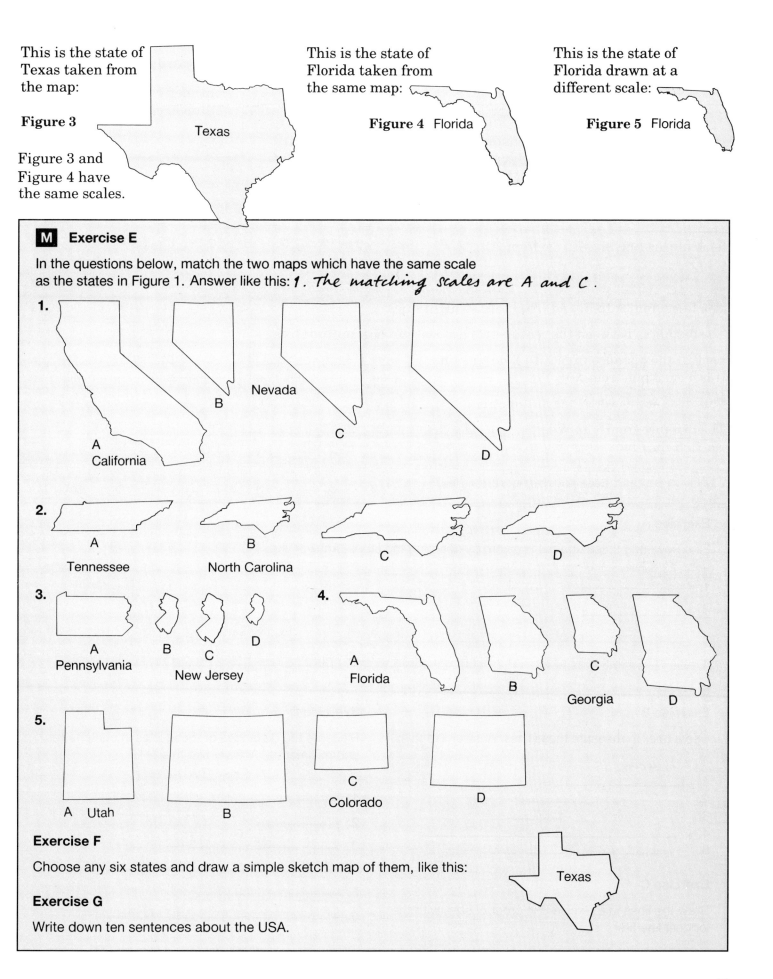

M **Exercise E**

In the questions below, match the two maps which have the same scale as the states in Figure 1. Answer like this: *1. The matching scales are A and C.*

1.
A California
B Nevada
C
D

2.
A Tennessee
B North Carolina
C
D

3.
A Pennsylvania
B C New Jersey D

4.
A Florida
B
C Georgia
D

5.
A Utah
B
C Colorado
D

Exercise F

Choose any six states and draw a simple sketch map of them, like this:

Texas

Exercise G

Write down ten sentences about the USA.

Measuring 1

Key words

centimetre   distance matrix
millimetre

One of the most important reasons for using a map may be to find out how far apart two places are. This unit shows you how to measure in different ways, for different reasons.

This distance is one **centimetre**:   It is 1 cm from A to B.

Look at this line. It is 10 cm from C to D.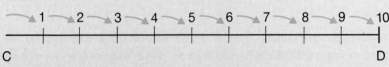

The lines from A to B, and C to D are straight lines.

The distances between the centimetres are measured in **millimetres**.

Look at the distance from X to Y on this line. It is 4 cm 3 mm from X to Y.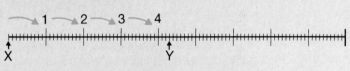

This distance is worth one millimetre: ⊣

The distance from V to W is worth 6 cm 7 mm.

Check these distances yourself with a ruler.

Exercise A

Find how long these straight lines are by counting the steps. Answer like this: *1. 5cm*

1.

2. ⊢——┼——┼——┤

3. ⊢——┼——┼——┼——┼——┼——┼——┤

4. ⊢——┼——┼——┼——┼——┼——┼——┼——┼——┼——┼——┤

5. ⊢——┼——┼——┼——┼——┼——┤

Exercise B

Use a ruler to measure these lines. Answer like this:

1. 4cm

1. _____

2. _____

3. _____

4. _____

5. _____

Exercise C

Draw the lines in Exercise B in order of size, with the longest line first.

Exercise D

Measure the distances of these lines in centimetres and millimetres. Answer like this:

1. 5cm 3mm

1. ┡━━━━┼━━━━┼━━━━┼━━━━┼━━┥

2. ┡━━━━┼━━━━┥

3. ┡━━━━┼━━━━┼━━━━┼━━━┥

4. ┡━━━━┼━━━━┼━━━━┼━━━━┼━━┥

5. ┡━━━━┼━━━━┼━━━┥

6. ┡━━━━┼━━━━┼━━━━┼━━━━┼━━┥

Look at this diagram.

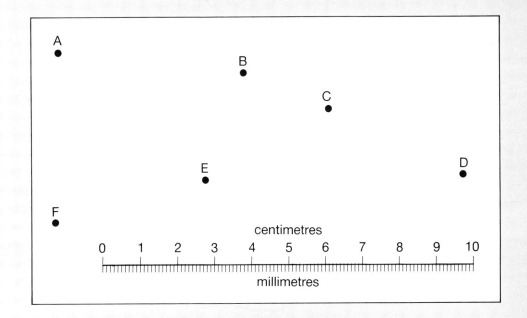

The distances between the dots can be measured by using a piece of paper. Like this:

Step 1

Place the straight edge of the paper along a line between the two dots. Like this:

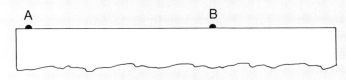

Step 2

Mark the paper to show where the centres of the dots are. Like this:

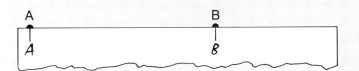

Step 3

Place the straight edge of the paper along the measuring line on the diagram. Like this:

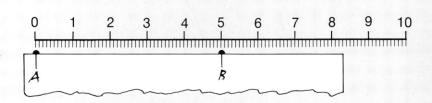

The distances can be set out in a chart. The chart is called a **distance matrix**.

This is a distance matrix. It shows the distance from A to B. You can also see it is 4 cm 5 mm from A to F, and 7 cm from D to E.

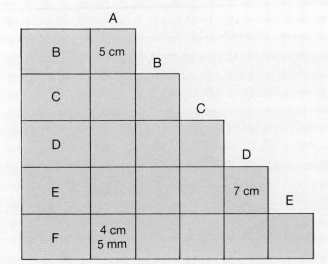

Exercise E

Copy and complete this distance matrix by measuring the distances between the dots.

Measuring 2

Sometimes you may need to measure a distance which is not in a straight line.

This section is about measuring curved distances.

Look at this curved line. It is 9 cm long.

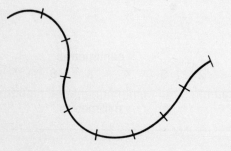

This straight line is also 9 cm long.

Both lines are worth the same distance. If you place string over the curved line and pull it straight, it will fit on the straight line. (Try it.)

M **Exercise A**

Match the curved lines with the straight lines.
Answer like this: *1. Line A and Line T are both 6 cm long.*

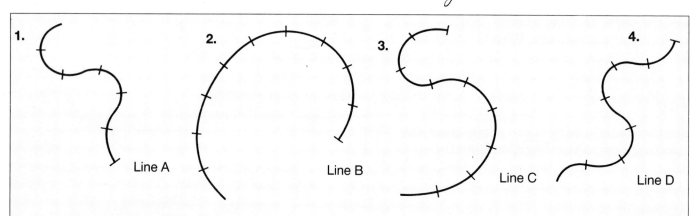

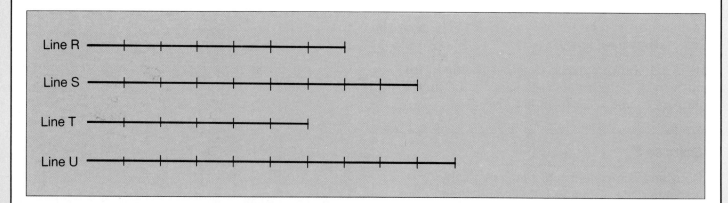

Look at the curved line from A to D. The straight lines from A to B, B to C, and C to D are almost the same shape.

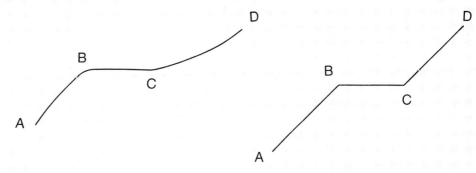

The lines A−B, B−C, and C−D can be measured. So can the curved line, like this:

Step 1
Mark off the distance from A to B:

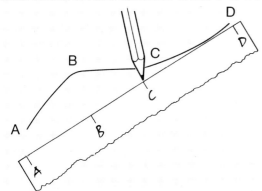

Step 2
Hold the paper down at B, using the point of your pencil, and mark off the distance from B to C:

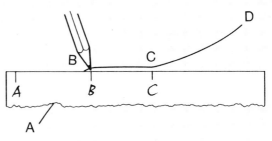

Step 3
Hold the paper down at C, using the point of your pencil. Mark off the distance from C to D.

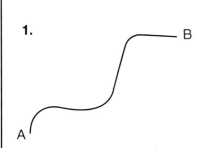

Step 4
Measure the distance from A to D on the paper.

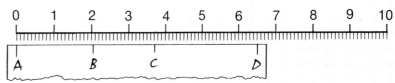

The distance from A to D is 6cm 5mm.

The length of a curved line cannot be measured exactly this way. But it will be very close to the exact length.

Exercise B

Measure the lengths of these curved lines, using paper, and the measuring line.

1.

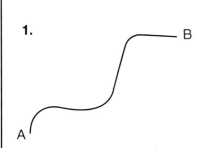

2.

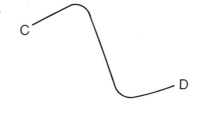

3.

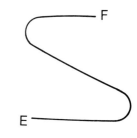

Measuring 3

This section is about measuring distances on maps.

The measuring line on a map is called a **scale line**.

Scale is the link between shape and size. Some maps of Great Britain are different in size, but they all have the same shape. They have different scales. The scale of a map is the way it has been reduced to fit on to the page.

These two maps show Great Britain, but they have different scales. The real distance between London and Edinburgh is always the same.

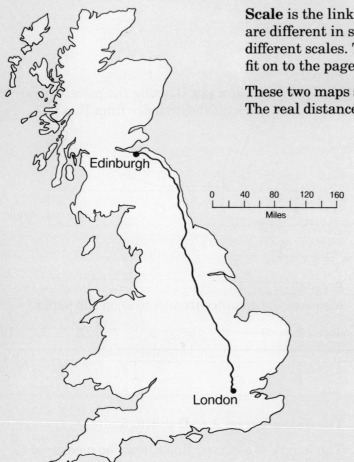

Figure 1 Great Britain

Figure 2 Great Britain

Exercise A

Look at Figure 1. Measure the distance in a straight line between London and Edinburgh, using the scale line.

Exercise B

Look at Figure 1. Measure the distance **by road** between London and Edinburgh.

Exercise C

What is the difference in miles between Exercises A and B?

Exercise D

Look at Figure 2. Measure the distance between London and Edinburgh, using the scale line.

Exercise E

Look at Figure 2. Measure the distance by road between London and Edinburgh.

Exercise F

Which map do you think shows the most accurate distance between London and Edinburgh. Why?

Exercise G

Measure the distance from London to Edinburgh, from Figure 3, in a straight line.

FG **Exercise H**

Copy and complete the sentences below, using Figure 3.
Measure the distances in a straight line.

1. London to Paris is _____ kilometres.
2. London to Rome is _____ kilometres.
3. London to Brussels is _____ kilometres.
4. London to Lisbon is _____ kilometres.
5. London to Bonn is _____ kilometres.
6. London to Amsterdam is _____ kilometres.
7. London to Stockholm is _____ kilometres.
8. London to Dublin is _____ kilometres.

Exercise I

Do Exercise H again,
but this time use Figure 4.

Figure 4

CH **Exercise J**

Copy and complete these sentences:

1. My answers in Exercises H and I should be (different / the same).
2. My answers in Exercises H and I (are / are not) the same.
3. My most accurate answers are those in (Exercise H / Exercise I).

Look at this map showing the capital cities in Europe:

Figure 3 Map of Western Europe showing capital cities

Measuring 4

This section is about measuring distances on small scale maps.

On some maps, the world has been reduced many times to fit on the paper. A small distance on the map can really mean thousands of kilometres.

Measuring distances accurately on these maps can be difficult.

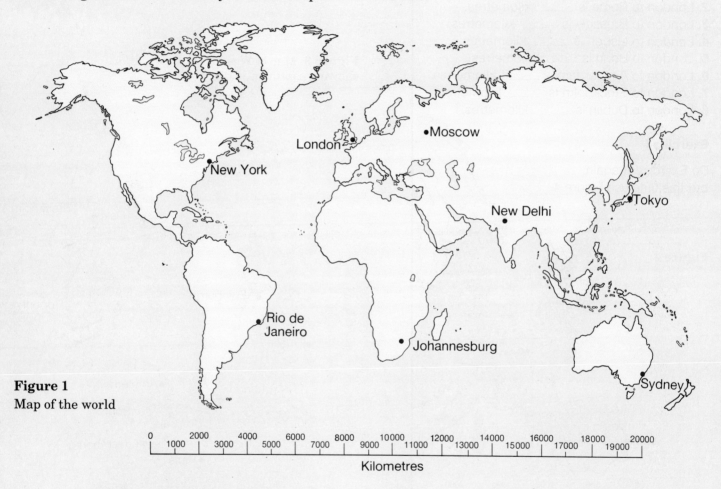

Figure 1
Map of the world

The scale line on the map shows distances every thousand kilometres. The distance between London and New York can be measured like this:

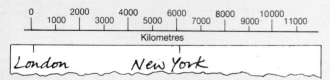

The distance between London and New York can be **rounded off** to 6000 kilometres. This means the distance is measured to the nearest thousand kilometres mark, on the scale line.

CH   **Exercise A**

Look at these distances and complete the sentences:

1. The distance between London and Johannesburg is about (5000 / 9000) kilometres.
2. The distance between London and Moscow is about (3000 / 4000) kilometres.
3. The distance between London and New Delhi is about (6000 / 7000) kilometres.

Exercise B

Look at these distances below, and **round them off** to the nearest hundred kilometres. Answer like this: *1. 200 kilometres*

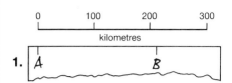
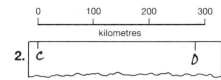
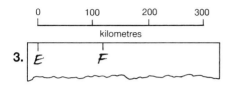

Exercise C

Look at these distances below. **Round off** the distances to the nearest thousand kilometres.

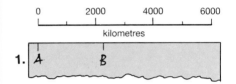
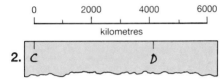
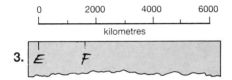

Exercise D

Round off these distances to the nearest **thousand miles**.

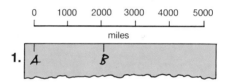
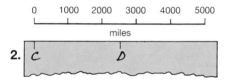
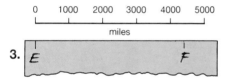

Exercise E

Round off these distances to the nearest hundred kilometres. Answer like this: *1. 500 kilometres*

1. 490 kilometres   **4.** 330 kilometres
2. 670 kilometres   **5.** 775 kilometres
3. 510 kilometres

Exercise F

Round off these distances to the nearest thousand kilometres. Like this: *1. 3000 kilometres*

1. 2970 kilometres   **4.** 8979 kilometres
2. 6750 kilometres   **5.** 1310 kilometres
3. 4002 kilometres

Exercise G

Look at the world map and complete this distance matrix. Measure distances to the nearest thousand kilometres. Like this:

	London	New York	Rio de Janeiro	Tokyo
New York	6000			
Rio de Janeiro				
Tokyo				
Sydney				

T   Exercise H

1. On a map of the British Isles, measure the distance between your town, and five other towns.
2. Round off all distances, to the nearest ten miles.
3. Draw a distance matrix for all six towns.

Graphs 1

Key words

diagrams   data
rainfall   survey

Sometimes in geography diagrams are used to show how things are related. These diagrams are called graphs. This unit shows you how to read and draw graphs.

Drawings and diagrams show things in a quick and simple way. They do not have to show a lot of writing.

A graph is a special kind of diagram. It shows how two things are related. Look at this bar graph.

The bar graph shows how much rain the city of Cardiff had for one year. It shows how rainfall and time are related.

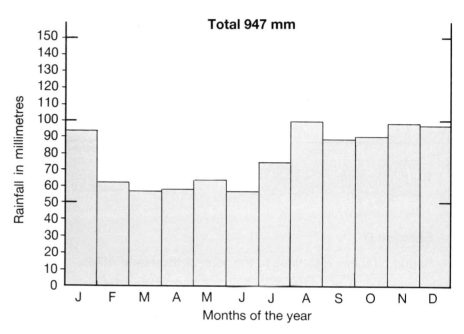

Figure 1   Bar graph showing rainfall for Cardiff

A bar graph is drawn inside a frame. The line going across the page is called the **horizontal axis**. The line going up the page is called the **vertical axis**.

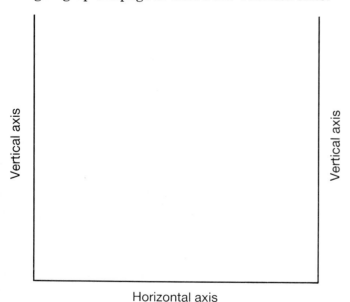

Figure 2 Bar graph frame

FG **Exercise A**

Look at the bar graph and write down how much rain fell in the following months. Answer like this:

1. January   = *94 mm*
2. July   = _____
3. December = _____
4. May   = _____
5. September = _____

Exercise B

Answer the questions below by naming the months. Answer like this: *1 August*

1. Name the wettest month.
2. Name the driest month.
3. Which month had 99 mm of rain?
4. Which month had 75 mm of rain?
5. Which months had less than 60 mm of rain?
6. Which months had more than 90 mm of rain?

How to draw a bar graph

The information needed to draw a graph is called **data**. The data below comes from a **survey**. A class were asked how they came to school each day. These are the results:

Method 1 by public transport 6 children
Method 2 by school coach   2 children
Method 3 by walking   10 children
Method 4 by car   8 children
Method 5 by bicycle   4 children

The class had to draw a bar graph to show these results. This is how they did it:

Step 1
Draw the vertical axis to show the number of children (the biggest number for any of the groups is 10). Draw the horizontal axis to show how children come to school (there are five methods).

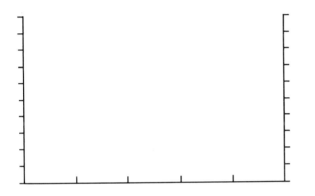

Step 2
Label the horizontal axis and the vertical axis. Give the graph a heading.

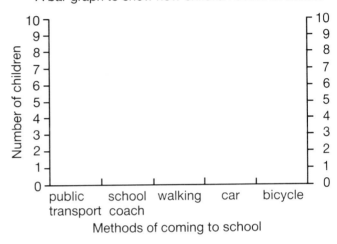

A bar graph to show how children come to school

Step 3
Draw bars on to the graph to show the results of the survey. Start like this:

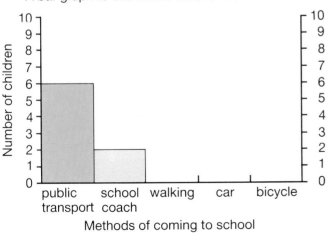

A bar graph to show how children come to school

Exercise C

1. Copy and complete the bar graph showing how the children come to school.
2. Write **two** sentences about what the graph shows.

Exercise D

Draw a bar graph for this set of data of rainfall in London.

Months	J	F	M	A	M	J	J	A	S	O	N	D
Rainfall in mm	49	43	48	41	46	52	60	55	47	64	56	61

T Exercise E

Carry out a survey of how children in your class come to school. Draw a bar graph to show the results, and explain what the graph shows.

page 73

Graphs 2

This section is about line graphs.
A line graph is another type of graph. It is often used to show temperature.

Look at this line graph. It shows the changes in temperature in one year for the city of Cardiff. These are **average** temperatures for each month. That means they show what it is like for most of the time.

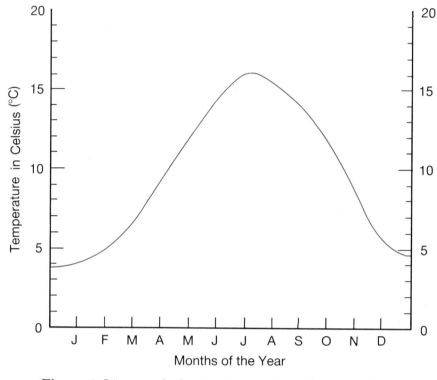

Figure 1 Line graph showing temperature for Cardiff

FG **Exercise A**

Look at the line graph and write down the average temperatures at the following times.
Answer like this:

1. January   = 4°C
2. July   = _____
3. December = _____
4. May   = _____
5. September = _____
6. August   = _____

Exercise B

Answer the questions below by naming the months.
Answer like this: 1. January

1. Name the coldest month.
2. Name the hottest month.
3. Which months had an average temperature of 11°C?
4. Which month had an average temperature of 16°C?
5. Which months had an average temperature between 5°C and 10°C?

T **Exercise C**

Keep a record of the temperatures in your school yard for one week. Set out your data like this:

Day 1	Day 2	Day 3	Day 4	Day 5
__°C	__°C	__°C	__°C	__°C
		Temperatures		

How to draw a line graph

A survey was made of the number of people using a supermarket at different times of the day. This is the data from the survey:

	1	2	3	4	5	6
Time	8–10 a.m.	10–12 a.m.	12–2 p.m.	2–4 p.m.	4–6 p.m.	6–8 p.m.
Number of people	50	150	180	100	250	150

How to draw a line graph of this data:

Step 1
Decide on the scale of the horizontal axis and the vertical axis. (There are six different times. The highest number of people is 250.)

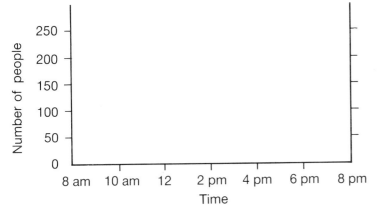

Step 2
Mark the number of people on to the graph, with a large dot. Put each dot in the centre of the times. Like this:

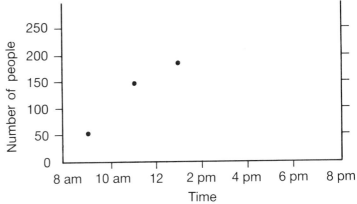

Step 3
Join the dots with a line and give the graph a heading. Like this:

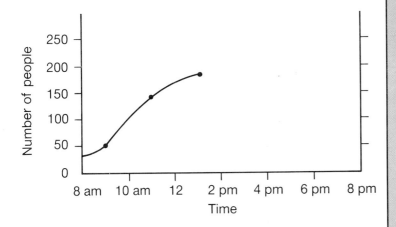

A line graph showing how many people use a supermarket

Exercise D

1. Copy and complete the line graph shown in Step 3.
2. Write three sentences about what the line graph shows.

Exercise E

1. Draw a line graph for your results for Exercise C.
2. Write two sentences about this graph.

Exercise F

Draw a line graph for these average temperatures.

Months	J	F	M	A	M	J	J	A	S	O	N	D
Temperatures (°C)	1	3	8	12	16	21	23	22	17	12	7	3

T **Exercise G**

1. Write down three surveys in your school that a line graph could be used for.
2. Draw a line graph for the data from one of these surveys.

Graphs 3

Key words

circle   continents
pie graph

This section looks at another kind of graph.

Look at these circles. They are all the same size. The red parts in each circle are all different sizes. The names of the parts are written under the circles.

 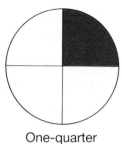 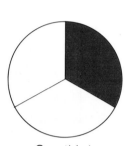 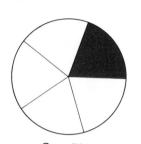 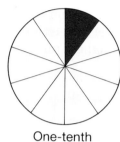

One-half   One-quarter   One-third   One-fifth   One-tenth

$\frac{1}{2}$ $\frac{1}{4}$ $\frac{1}{3}$ $\frac{1}{5}$ $\frac{1}{10}$

The circles are another type of graph.

This type of graph is called a pie graph, because each part looks like a piece from a pie.

Exercise A

Look at the pie graphs below, and write down how much is coloured green, in words and numbers.
Answer like this: *1. A quarter, ¼*

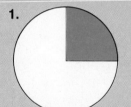   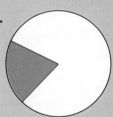 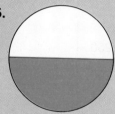

1.   **2.**   **3.**   **4.**   **5.**

Exercise B

Look at the pie graphs below and write down how much is coloured green, in words and numbers. Answer like this. *1. Two-thirds, 2/3*

 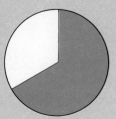 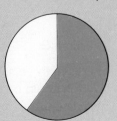 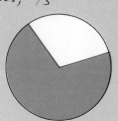 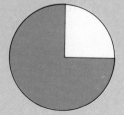

1.   **2.**   **3.**   **4.**

This pie graph shows the size of the continents.

Figure 1 Pie graph showing size of continents

The largest continent is Asia. This map shows the main countries in South-East Asia.

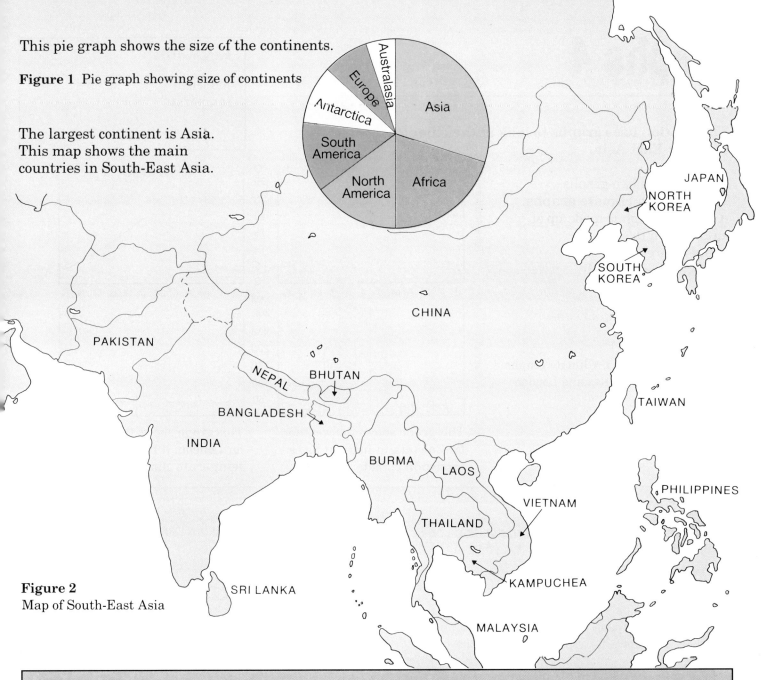

Figure 2
Map of South-East Asia

FG **Exercise C**

Look at the pie graph above, and copy and complete the sentences below.
Like this:

1. Asia covers about ⅓ of the world.
2. Africa covers about _____ of the world.
3. Antarctica covers about _____ of the world.
4. South America covers about _____ of the world.
5. Europe covers about _____ of the world.

Exercise D

Look at the pie graph above, and list the continents in order of size. Start with the largest continent.

Exercise E

Look at the pie graph below showing the sizes of some of the countries in South-East Asia. Write five sentences about the sizes of the countries shown on the graph:

T **Exercise F**

On an outline map of South-East Asia mark in the names of the countries shown in the pie graph.

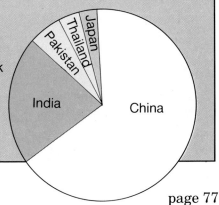

Graphs 4

This section uses graphs to look at the climate
of South-East Asia.

Look at these two graphs.
They are both **climate graphs**.
A climate graph is made up of
a line graph to show
temperature, and a bar
graph to show rainfall.

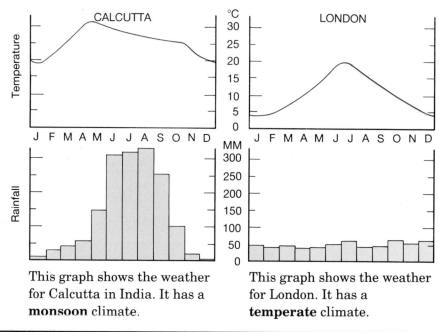

Figure 1 Climate graphs
for Calcutta and London

This graph shows the weather
for Calcutta in India. It has a
monsoon climate.

This graph shows the weather
for London. It has a
temperate climate.

FG Exercise A

Look at the climate graph for Calcutta, and copy
and complete these sentences. Like this:

1. The wettest month is *August*.
2. The driest month is _____ .
3. The rainfall in November is _____ mm.
4. The rainfall in July is _____ mm.
5. Calcutta has _____ mm of rainfall in one year.

FG Exercise B

Look at the climate graph for London, and copy and
complete these sentences.

1. The wettest month is _____ .
2. The driest month is _____ .
3. The rainfall in November is _____ mm.
4. The rainfall in July is _____ mm.
5. London has _____ mm of rainfall in one year.

FS Exercise C

Look at the climate graph for Calcutta and
complete these sentences.

1. The hottest month is _____ .
2. The coldest month is _____ .
3. The temperature in May is _____ °C.
4. The temperature in December is _____ °C.

FS Exercise D

Look at the climate graph for London and complete
these sentences.

1. The hottest month is _____ .
2. The coldest month is _____ .
3. The temperature in May is _____ °C.
4. The temperature in December is _____ °C.

Exercise E

Read your answers for Exercises A–D. Write five
sentences about the main differences between a
monsoon climate and a temperate climate.

Exercise F

Describe what the weather in Britain is like at these
times of year:

1. December to March.
2. June to December.

This map shows the areas of South-East Asia which have a monsoon climate.

From December to March it is dry and cool. From March to May it is very hot and very dry; the air is still and uncomfortable. Then suddenly the rains come, and there are heavy storms, with very strong winds.

Figure 2 Map of monsoon areas in South-East Asia

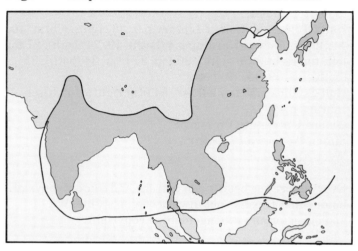

Figures 3 and 4 show that the rains come when the winds suddenly change direction.

Figure 3

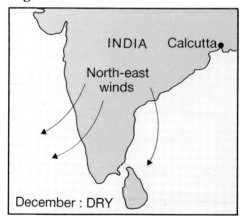

Figure 4

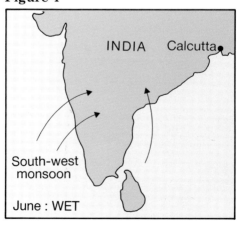

FG **Exercise G**

Copy and complete these sentences, using the words below, and Figures 3 and 4.

The climate in South-East Asia is called a _____ climate. In December winds come from the _____ to the sea. This means they are _____ winds. In June they come from the _____ . These winds bring heavy _____ .

dry / monsoon / land / rain / sea

Exercise H

Use the map above, and the map on page 77, to name the countries which have a monsoon climate.

Exercise I

1. Describe what you can see in the two photographs.
2. Write down when you think the photographs were taken and say how you know.

Exercise J

What do you think are the main problems caused by a monsoon climate? Give reasons to explain your answer.

Acknowledgements

The publishers and author would like to thank the following people for their permission to use copyright material:

Ardea p.27 btm left, 28 left, 29, 31 top, 32, 33, 54 top right, top left, btm left;
Daily Telegraph Colour Library p.9, 28 right, 30btm, 40, 44, 49, 55; Robert Harding p.4 (both), 19, 24 (both), 27 top left, top right, btm right,, 30 top, 31 btm, 34 (both), 35 (both), 38, 39, 45, 79 (both);
Holt Studios p.37 top left, 48, 54 btm right; Hutchison Library p.41;
Oxford University Press p.58;
Simon Warner p.17 (both);
West Air p.36, 62.

Every effort has been made to trace and contact copyright holders but this has not always been possible. We apologise for any infringement of copyright.